DERBY

David Whish-Wilson is the author of the Frank Swann series of crime novels set in 1970s and '80s Perth, and the *Perth* book in the NewSouth Books city series. His most recent novel is *Old Scores* (Fremantle Press, 2016). He lives in Fremantle and coordinates the creative writing program at Curtin University.

Sean Gorman has studied and worked in the Indigenous studies field for twenty-three years. He currently holds a senior fellowship at Curtin University. Gorman's work draws on social justice, social history, sports history, and local history. He is the lead investigator on the recently completed ARC linkage grant entitled *Assessing the Australian Football League's Racial and Religious Vilification Laws to Promote Community Harmony, Multiculturalism and Reconciliation.* His book *Brotherboys: The Story of Jim and Phillip Krakouer* was adapted for a play and had a national tour in 2011. His latest book *Legends: The AFL Indigenous Team of the Century* came out in 2011.

WA FOOTY FANS ON THE GAME'S GREATEST RIVALRY

DAVID WHISH-WILSON & SEAN GORMAN

to our footballing fathers –
Peter Gorman and Tony Whish-Wilson

Aboriginal and Torres Strait Islander people are respectfully advised that deceased people may be referenced in this publication.

FOREWORD – DENNIS COMETTI

A faded poster hangs on the wall of my gym at home. It features rival captains John Worsfold and Ben Allan (predominantly in green) competing for a mark under a boldly typed message: THE STATE IS DIVIDED. IT'S NOT LIFE OR DEATH, IT'S MORE IMPORTANT. In retrospect, that poster seems like a battle cry of hype and hope. Hype to whip up interest, and the hope that somehow a real rivalry could rise out of such lopsided beginnings. Through the summer of 1994–95, I'd never seen two clubs less likely to fan a rivalry than West Coast and Fremantle.

Geography aside, in competitive terms it was a mismatch of massive proportions. The Eagles under Michael Malthouse were coming off their third grand final in four years and a second premiership. They were the benchmark of the AFL. By stark contrast the Dockers had been cobbled together over a few months. Their coach, Gerard Neesham, was untried beyond the WAFL. West Coast was laden with stars. Names like Jakovich, Matera, Kemp, Mainwaring, McKenna, Heady, Sumich, Worsfold and Turley were the stuff of legend. In 1995, the Eagles read like a *Who's Who* of the competition. By contrast, Fremantle fans could only look at their list and ask, 'Who's he?' Of all the new clubs before or since, none were given fewer player concessions than the Dockers. The only blessing the rookie club had was that it could look across the river at the reigning premier. There could be no mistaking the height of the bar!

The two clubs met for the first time on May 14 in round seven. And against all the odds, Fremantle arrived at that match in remarkable shape. Picked by most experts to go through the season winless, they had won three of their first six games. More to the point, their three losses were by a combined total of just sixteen points. But it was a record that stood for nought. On that warm Sunday afternoon, Malthouse's men ruthlessly marked out their turf. Brett Heady put on a clinic as Fremantle was in turn outmuscled then outhustled. The old adage that a great team still 'put their pants on one leg at a time' was put to rest very early. Within minutes it was abundantly clear to every Docker that their opposition wore considerably bigger pants and that they put them on a good deal faster. The Eagles won that first derby by eighty-five points. They went on to win the next eight.

The magic of this rivalry is not that it survived such domination but that it thrived. In time, the Eagles lost many of their champions and then in round ten, 1999, they finally lost to Fremantle. In the seasons to the end of 2016, the Dockers have won twenty of the forty-four games played. During this impressive run, the Dockers produced their own legends – players like Matthew Pavlich, Peter Bell, Aaron Sandilands, Nathan Fyfe and David Mundy. Nowadays the mere mention of a Western Derby raises a smile anywhere around Australia. A smile that acknowledges an edge that few games have. So much so that, in 2015, the prospect of a Western Derby AFL grand final was eagerly anticipated by many people outside Western Australia. Given the decline of Victorian powerhouse clubs like Essendon, Carlton and Collingwood, the Eagles–Dockers rivalry is the best in the AFL. It is testimony that rivalries are more about what they become than how they begin.

CONTENTS

Foreword – Dennis Cometti 5
Introduction – David Whish-Wilson & Sean Gorman 9

Derby Teams 13
David Wirrpanda – Eagles 14
Shaun McManus – Dockers 20
Dennis Lillee – Eagles 28
Maria Giglia – Dockers 33
Gillian O'Shaughnessy – Dockers 38
Matt Quinn aka Mr Q – Eagles 43
Fedele Camarda – Dockers 48
Kim Scott – Dockers 54
Ross McLean – Dockers 59
Kevin Croon – Dockers 66
Greig Johnston – Eagles 72
Maria Camporeale – Dockers 78
Ron Elliott – Eagles 83
Justin Langer – Eagles 88
Gaby Haddow – Eagles 94
Melissa Parke – Dockers 99
Julie Bishop – Eagles 104
Parsi – Eagles 109
Ian MacRae – Eagles 115
Alison Fan – Dockers 121
James Baker – Eagles 126
Glen Stasiuk – Eagles 132

Bevan Taylor – Eagles 137
Alsy Macdonald – Dockers 142
Deanne Lewis – Dockers 147
Jesse Dart – Dockers 151
Kia Mippy – Eagles 155
Glenis Freemantle – Dockers 159
Janet Peters – Eagles 163
Carla Mackesey – Eagles 167
Lesley the Voodoo Lady – Dockers 172
Jeff Newman – Eagles 177
Les Everett – Dockers 182
Luc Longley – Dockers 187
Bill Sutherland – Eagles 191
John Prior – Dockers 196
Clive Mercer – Dockers 201
Mark Greenwood – Eagles 206
Julie & Adrian Hoffman – Eagles 210
Peter Mudie – Dockers 214

Western Derbies 220
Biggest Winning and Losing Margins 222
Coaches 223
Ross Glendinning Medallists 224

Contributors 225
Acknowledgements 239

INTRODUCTION – DAVID WHISH-WILSON & SEAN GORMAN

Football, it has been said many times, is more than a game. Perhaps the reason for this is that it intersects, overlaps and pervades so many different sectors of society. Those who follow the code enter into a broad church where the language of the game, its myths, its long narrative arcs, its champions, its villains and its seasonal rhythms bind us together regardless of who we follow. Here we stand around the water cooler, talking about footy tipping or the latest footy scandal; then there's Facebook footy chat, emails, texts, posts … it goes on ad infinitum.

Our football allegiances define us and, in turn, they determine the types of interactions we have with others. You know what we are talking about: the taxi driver who goes for Freo and doesn't mind telling you about it all the way from Midland to Mandurah; the crazy neighbour who lives in Fremantle but goes for the Eagles; the butcher who has the Eagles premiership teams framed and hanging on the shop wall beside a shrine to the Madonna; the pesky kid over the fence who goes for Freo and whose purple ball ends up in your yard; and the lady at reception who has a lolly jar on her desk full of yellow and blue Smarties that she delights in offering Dockers fans. One-eyed, hard-boiled, rusted-on, staunch. Why? The psychic space that football has in our lives can be reduced to a few potent drivers, especially when it comes to the teams we follow: love, loyalty, admiration. The genesis of these drivers can come from all manner of things: a grainy game on TV on a cold afternoon; listening to a memorable match in your high-school dorm; having a favourite uncle or aunt foist a guernsey on you as a child; or the chance encounter with a football star down at the local deli or bottle shop. They are moments where fate steps in and, before you know it, you are riding the bumps with a grin.

Once we don the colours and the totem of our team, we go deeper into the age-old notion of what being in a tribe must have been like. We define who we are by what we are not. We dispense with the tool of reason and all of the justifications and arguments that are important to everyday life, and instead fall back on ancient human traits that don't need to be tested, such as loyalty and stubborn belief: footy as a secular religion. We become absorbed in the always-developing human drama and sometimes comic theatre of our team and the game that we love. We become experts and pundits and sages and disciples of the inexact and mysterious forces that guide the fate of our club, and therefore our lives. Because we live it week to week, and game to game, we understand in our bones the words of French philosopher Albert Camus, when he claimed that what he knew most surely about morality he learned from playing and watching sport – the ethics of sticking up for your friends, your team, your community, and valuing courage and perseverance and fair play and respect for those who oppose you. This latter feature as it applies to football rivalry is understandably the most difficult to sustain – in this case the difficulty many Dockers and Eagles fans have comprehending and articulating why others follow the 'mob up (or down) the road'. Time and again we've all heard it: 'How could they?', 'Why do they?', 'What's wrong with them?' And yet, despite this natural confusion – which in its turn shines a light on the complexities of human behaviour – we all place others and judge them by who they follow. This notion becomes acute when the rivalry boils down further to the best football rivalry in the land – that between the Fremantle Dockers and the West Coast Eagles. This gives rise to the Western Derby, and just about every Western Australian has an opinion on that.

We initially saw the idea of writing this book about the Western Derby as a chance to have some fun delving into the weird and wonderful thoughts of fans who could not stand the thought of the opposition. It would be a bit of a 'kick and a giggle', we thought. But what soon became apparent through the interviews was that this book was much more. It opened us to deep insights about what football means, and has meant, to Western Australians for decades. It is about social memory and local heritage, about deep passion for family and community forged on cold windy flanks at Leederville, Bassendean and Fremantle ovals. Of country footy, amateurs, school footy and backyard kick-to-kick, to wagging school for classic 1980s State of Origin football, to the Sunday night ritual of watching *The Winners* straight after *Countdown.* It is about great speccies and goals, and biffs, bombs and bullshit. It's about what attracts us to our teams and our favourite players. It's about what keeps our loyalty and (clubs, take note) what diminishes it. It was from this primordial football soup that the modern derby rivalry has emerged, and the antipathy between Dockers and Eagles fans seeps its way into each of these stories, with biting humour, begrudging respect, pathos and, in some cases, voodoo. As a broad story, this book contains some key themes, namely the importance of the many great Indigenous players who have shaped the game, and earned our respect and admiration. Another common theme is the importance of the WAFL to Western Australian cultural life, in terms of instilling the virtues and the tribalism that would later become focused on the two AFL derby rivals.

As well, the importance of a strongly felt sense of place, and of belonging, based around the suburbs and schools and landmarks of our city and state, and in turn how that sense of place and loyalty is purified by competitive feelings towards the perceived arrogance and dismissiveness encapsulated in the word 'Victorian'.

Derby rivalry is the bridging subject of this book, but its method lies in communicating the stories of the individuals who generously agreed to participate. We looked for a broad cross-section of our society – people from all walks of life who have something interesting to say. Sporting celebrities for their insights into the game and the power of their personal stories. Politicians and schoolteachers. Crayfishermen and nurses. Small-business owners and musicians. Artists and academics. Lawyers and farmers. Two teams of fans who have nominated their field positions based on their personalities and favourite numbers, each team with a captain (Shaun McManus and David Wirrpanda, whose physical clash in derby number thirteen has gone down in the annals of folklore as being perhaps the epitome of the derby rivalry – it even had Clive Waterhouse in it.) We thank our captains and all those who agreed to be interviewed, those who facilitated introductions and those who spent time with us.

For us, the derby is a social phenomenon that allows us to unpack so much about what it means to be Western Australian and why we follow the teams we do. It provides us with a starting point for a conversation so that other conversations may be had. Despite who we may go for, and the tribe we have chosen, or has chosen us, we can be assured that the game in Western Australia is alive and well, and regardless of who we go for, Western Australia really is the home of football.

DERBY TEAMS

Captains	David Wirrpanda (13), Shaun McManus (8)
FB	Julie & Adrian Hoffman (27, 18), Janet Peters (24), Bill Sutherland (28)
FF	Les Everett (22), Alison Fan (7), Lesley the Voodoo Lady (6)
HB	Ron Elliott, Jeff Newman (13), Mark Greenwood (7)
HF	Ross McLean (7), Kevin Croon (7), Maria Camporeale (13)
M	Greig Johnston (13), Justin Langer (9), Glen Stasiuk (2),
M	Glenis Freemantle (7), Kim Scott (13), Alsy Macdonald (4)
HF	Carla Mackesey (9), Julie Bishop (9), Ian McRae (6)
HB	Fedele Camarda (4), Melissa Parke (29), Clive Mercer (10)
FF	Matt Quinn (19), James Baker (9), Gaby Haddow (3)
FB	Maria Giglia, Luc Longley (13), Jesse Dart (1)
Followers	Bevan Taylor (30), Dennis Lillee (10), Parsi (2)
	John Prior (3), Peter Mudie (33), Deanne Lewis (28)
Supersub	Gillian O'Shaughnessy
Coach	Kia Mippy

DAVID WIRRPANDA – EAGLES

For David Selwyn Burralung Merringwuy Galarrwuy Wyal Wirrpanda, football has been good. Having played 227 AFL games for the West Coast Eagles, culminating in the one-point grand final win over Sydney in 2006, Wirrpanda – or 'Wirra' as he is more commonly known – has worked hard to establish the foundation that bears his name. In 2007 he was named by *The Bulletin* as one of Australia's most influential Aboriginal people, and in 2009 he was awarded the Young Western Australian of the Year. Such was the power of his brand that he was a contestant on *Dancing With the Stars*, and he even had a tilt in the 2013 federal election as the National Party's senate candidate for Western Australia. At his North Perth home we are not only greeted by Wirra but two employees and old Dockers adversaries in Dale Kickett and Troy Cook. The banter ensues about derby rivalry and games won and lost, but Wirrapanda focuses on what he first thought of the derby, having come from Victoria where he had witnessed hundred-year-old hostilities firsthand.

'Well, as a young bloke I didn't really understand the Western Derby because, being a Victorian, we had a derby every week in Melbourne. You know, the great rivalry between Carlton and Collingwood, Essendon and Richmond. I was a mad Hawthorn supporter so there were some pretty hot contests. That's why I wore 44 – because I was a Johnny Platten fan. I played on him when I was sixteen and didn't know whether to tackle him or kiss him. So when I heard about this *derby*, and the rivalry, it didn't really click until I was here. I started in '96 and I was pretty keen to see the Fremantle Dockers because they were the new franchise and they had a lot of Indigenous players. I remember watching Scotty Chisholm in the warm-up one day and thought he was pretty good. Then in round one in 1996, I got a little bit of an understanding of it, straight up.'

It didn't take Wirrpanda long to understand the importance of the derby game in the context of local football. 'I've got a really good understanding of the derby rivalry. I think the passion is huge, considering for a long time the majority of supporters were West Coast and now after more than twenty years I think it's almost fifty-fifty. That's exciting for Western Australian footy because Fremantle are now a serious contender. They're not there to be pushed around anymore by the so-called big brother. To their credit they have clawed their way back, and football in this state has been the winner.'

Wirrpanda had an intimate insight into the inner workings of the Eagles and he is refreshingly honest about what a derby means from a player's point of view. 'We used to be very diplomatic when it came to the derby, and we were gently instructed to make sure that we used the old clichés. But to be honest, it's a rivalry, you don't want them to win regardless of where you are on the ladder. It's as simple as that. There's nothing better than making sure that you're number one in the state. If we lose, we feel the heat. Like when you go up North, the majority of Kimberley people are all mad West Coast, and after a derby loss you get: "What's wrong with you? What happened?" You feel terrible because you've just let everyone down. The players all shake hands afterward but we couldn't stand each other, and that's the truth.'

Having taken some time to ease himself into the demands of the elite AFL competition, Wirrpanda recalls his first derby. 'I think my first real derby was in '99, and from there

I played a fair bit of them, but I got a real taste for it when John Worsfold was our captain. He made it very clear he did not want to lose to those blokes down the road and that was the rule of thumb.' Wirrpanda recalls that his first derby coincided with the first Dockers win, and it's not a pleasant memory. 'I just remember how gutted I was. I was playing on Brad Wira. He was tagging me for the day, and he got on top of me by kicking three goals. It was massive, like a final. To their credit they just kept clawing and clawing and eventually it was going to happen because it's just part and parcel of footy. It took me more than a week or two to get over it.'

Wirrpanda is quick to point out that there were times when the boot was on the other foot. 'If you really want to be successful you have to have a little bit of arrogance about you. Don't get me wrong. I'm a respectful person. My mum used to tell me to be fair and play the ball. I don't know if that makes sense, but that's what we tried to do – to keep the lid on things and not blow them out of proportion. The wins were great and felt good, because I wanted their players to remember me for next time. But you can't relax. They are tough games.'

Asked to describe how Wirrpanda and his team mates prepared for a big derby game, he replies, 'I know people like Dean Kemp really set himself for a big day with the derby. Brett Heady was another one. Glen Jakovich used to really fire up. Non-stop talking, geeing us up. Some blokes would spend the entire morning spewing up. I was relaxed, if anything too relaxed. Sometimes it used to annoy Woosha that I was a little bit too laidback. But I'd try to avoid that pressure of thinking about it a lot. I'd sit in the spa just before the game, have a yarn and a laugh. I wanted to make sure I was not wasting any energy and could come in fresh. But as soon as the siren went I'd go one hundred miles an hour.' Apart from trying to calm himself before a big match,

Wirrpanda's other concern before a big game was 'making sure my family had tickets. A few times in the warm-up, our boot-studder at the Eagles would walk in and say we have got your family here, and they want tickets, and I was literally just about to run through the banner. That was the thing that I used to stress over more. So I would make sure there was always a few spares at the door, because I didn't want them coming in to the change rooms humbugging me just as I was running out.'

During the week in the lead-up to a derby game, Wirrpanda often spent time training with Phil Matera as he prepared for playing on his toughest Fremantle opponent – The Wiz. 'Mate, Jeff Farmer was the toughest to play on by a country mile. I mean he was one of those players that I used to prepare myself for, and I didn't get a lot of sleep the night before. He knew the way I played, and I knew the way he played. We had really good battles and I think he's probably the best Docker I've played on. I would train really hard with Phil Matera in small spaces especially in the goal square. The only thing that The Wiz probably had over Phil is he could jump on your head. You'd keep him quiet all game and in two minutes he'd kick four on you. I'd yarn with him and have a bit of a laugh and ask about his family. We used to rotate different players on him. Drew Banfield was unbelievable as far as locking down on players, and Daniel Chick was good because he would get Jeff Farmer upset. I'd kind of take over from there and hold on because it was always a wild ride with The Wiz.'

The conversation shifts from that contest to perhaps the most bone-jarring incident to have occurred in derby history – the clash between Shaun McManus and Wirra in derby thirteen, 2001. Wirrpanda takes a sip of his coffee and looks off into the distance. He breathes in slowly and lets out a thoughtful sigh. 'That clash with Shauny Mac is probably my favourite memory in footy. It's up there with the grand final. Fremantle were breaking in the play and my mate Andrew Shipp, had the ball. I knew his kicks are not that accurate. He lobbed this kick and I saw Shauny Mac probably about ten metres behind me over my right shoulder, and I just remember thinking, "I'm quick enough to get to where the footy will be." I left my man and the footy was in the air. I was confident I was going to get there, mark it and take off. We were both watching the footy and running full lick and then I felt his jaw on my shoulder and the way I hit him it jolted my neck and I felt a bit unwell. I just remember getting up, and Peter Matera saying it's not a mark, and then Cookie had me by the throat. I was immediately concerned. I thought, "Jeez, he's seriously hurt," because Shauny's eyes were at the back of his head. He got the free, and was probably the worst kick in that team, and he's had a shot at goal and kicked it.Great memories, of a hard contest with one of Freo's favourite sons.'

Despite the derby ledger being so in favour of the Eagles for so many years, the outcome of having regular highly competitive games has seen the win–loss ratio even up and both teams have benefitted. 'Once we played regular derbies you could see players really develop from Freo's end, as well as ours. I mean there was myself, Ben Cousins, Chad Morrison, Michael Braun and Rowan Jones. Then you saw players like Paul Haselby and Matthew Pavlich really start to push and make a name for themselves, not just for Fremantle but in the AFL. And that's where the respect starts to grow, because the rivalry grows too. Now these retired players are some of the most popular, and it's important for me and for the boys as well to keep that relationship, because they were pretty big servants for the footy club. I encourage all the Aboriginal players that work for me to keep up relationships with their old clubs.'

Wirrpanda, Cook and Kickett have to head off to the airport where they have a scheduled meeting. We ask Wirra whether there will ever be a derby grand final. 'Well, we almost had one in 2006. I think that was probably the closest we've been, but the potential between both the football clubs now to play in the GF is a lot closer than we think, whether it's this year, or maybe another year or two down the track. But I'm worried about the changeover of the squads. That's probably to Freo's detriment that they're going to have a big changeover in the next couple of years. We all saw what happened when the Eagles lost Matera, Kemp, Jakovich, McKenna, Worsfold, and we had that big dip down the bottom. It's a process that Freo are dealing with now. But both footy clubs are really well managed with fresh blood, new ideas, different coaches, different structures, and I think they're going to be a lot more successful, but I would love to see a derby grand final.'

SHAUN McMANUS – DOCKERS

It was one of the pivotal moments in derby games thus far. Like everything with football, it happened very fast, and yet for many it's remembered in slow motion. The scores were pretty much level in derby number thirteen, 2001, when Andrew Shipp took the ball forward for the Dockers, and Shaun McManus ran towards the goal to intercept the pass. Forty-five thousand fans were screaming, and all McManus heard was 'complete silence. Complete silence, because your concentration is so intense – you're completely immersed in the game.'

The kind of silence McManus describes illustrates the mental toughness of an elite athlete, but with an added element more specific to the game of football. The silence he experienced as he reached for the airborne pass also blocked out the sound of *footsteps* – a sound that when heard, and acted upon, can tarnish a player's career for life.

But nobody has ever accused Shaun McManus of shirking or cowardice, and what happened next exemplifies the attitude of a player many consider to be Fremantle's most loyal clubman, and fiercest derby competitor – a man whose heart, according to many, 'bleeds purple'. 'I don't think I was playing too well at that time. I remember we got a run on in a passage of play and the ball ended up with Andrew Shipp, just outside the fifty-metre line. At that stage I was just trying to will myself into the game – I was hell-bent on streaming into open space in the forward line. I just needed to get the ball – I was desperate to get a touch to get myself back into the game. When Andrew popped the ball over the top I just kept running and it didn't occur to me that another player might be running the other way. It didn't bother me because I was desperate to be part of the game, instead of floating around on the edges, so I went hard for the ball and got absolutely nailed. I didn't know what the bloody hell happened. I was just lying on the ground and had no idea what was going on. My head was all over the place, and I was breathing hard.'

Trainers went to McManus's aid, but it wasn't them who got him to his feet. 'The thing that jogged me back to reality was Clive Waterhouse, who told me to stay down so he could take the kick. And I was like, "You're not taking the kick." So that got me up, I was on the boundary line, and thought back to my basic training. I used to take three steps and jog in with the ball, and I did that and it went straight through. Everyone came up and jumped all over me, but if you look at my face, I wasn't all with it. I was thinking, "Holy shit, I'm cooked." But it's funny how clear the rest of the day became. I ended up having a great game, with twenty-eight possessions and three goals, although we lost the match.'

McManus was born into an arm of the broader Regan and Neesham clans, whose names are synonymous with Fremantle, and Fremantle football history. He grew up in Willeton, and in and around Shark Park, the home of East Fremantle. 'I was pretty lucky because my grandpa, Jack McManus, he worked down here at Shark Park as a player welfare manager. He had a lot to do with players coming down from Geraldton, like Mainwaring and Murray Wrensted, and in all the team photos from the '80s you'll see him in there. He'd bring players back to his house, and they'd all be there for our big family Sunday dinners, and when we'd come down to Shark Park he'd take us into the change rooms. All the players knew him, and to me he was an extremely famous person. My cousins and I were all passionate about footy, because we were able to go to the games. Like other kids, we would fight to get the ball after it went through the goal, fight to get it and then kick it back onto the oval, and then we'd change ends depending on who the full-forward was for East Fremantle – I remember one game when Darren Bennett kicked something like twenty goals for East Freo in the reserves. We'd also get cardboard boxes and slide down the back of the hills there, and after the game when everyone cleared out, me and my brother walked around the oval collecting the footy *Budget*s, which had a 'buy one get one free' Whopper voucher inside. We'd load them up and take them home. So it was a magical place to come to.'

Growing up following East Fremantle meant that derby rivalry was instilled in Shaun from an early age. 'I don't remember having *any* friends who followed South Fremantle, except for one who, as a European mate, was attracted to the Italian element of Souths. For us you just hated South Fremantle. When I started playing colts aged sixteen, from day one we were told, "This is how it is – we hate these guys," and it was pumped into you constantly. It was like a cult, we were brainwashed into it. It didn't matter – win, lose or draw, if the derby was next week we'd be straight into it, it was always the club's most important game.'

Shaun's first league game for the Sharks was against the archenemy, at Fremantle Oval. 'We all caught the bus together, even though it's what … a hundred metres down the road? Just so we could go into the ground together. Allan Jeans, the legendary Hawthorn coach, was there because of our coach Ken Judge, and he gave a memorable speech: "It's not the size of the dog in the fight, but the size of the fight in the dog." He really pumped it into me and I was able to get out there and get a few kicks and I really enjoyed it. It was a huge day. Souths had the Collard brothers playing, and people like Peter Bell, Peter Matera and Craig Edwards, the Sandover Medallist. After the game we went straight back to Shark Park. We didn't have a shower there or anything, because we were always told, "Ah, they'll turn the hot water off," or something like that. Back at our clubrooms, they had a stage and a bit of a walkway, and I remember as a kid watching the players say a few words, and now it was my turn, this young kid getting introduced to the crowd.'

When the Eagles entered the competition, Shaun, like many other West Australians, began to follow West Coast 'because it was seen as a WA team. I used to watch a fair few of their games, but when they started to become successful there started to be talk of a port team. When the whispers began about Fremantle joining the competition, there was no way I was going to play for anyone else.'

Being drafted as a teenager into the first Dockers team was a surreal experience. 'We had Gerard Neesham as our coach, and he taught me a model of play that was exciting. But also, instead of Mum buying my boots, who could never afford it, all of a sudden a guy from Nike would turn up at training, and you could pick as many pairs as you wanted. It was just ridiculous – they gave you all these clothes, and free boots, and cartons of Emu Export, because Swan Brewery was a sponsor and I thought, "This is unbelievable," but then training started and that made you think, "Shit, this is *real*." You started to flog yourself to get to the next level.'

Shaun's first game for the Dockers was against the Western Bulldogs in round five of 1995, 'and my heart was pumping, I felt like I ran faster because I was playing against these blokes I'd only seen on *The Winners*, and the crowd was feral, it was pretty full-on. I didn't feel like I belonged, at that point, although I had a good game, and it became an obsession to get to the level to be considered an AFL player.'

Two weeks later was the inaugural Eagles–Dockers derby. 'It was easy for me to find the passion, although I don't think that was across the board. I'd played WAFL derbies in Fremantle, and I was a Fremantle person; we came together as a group of misfits in a way, and we were trying to hang onto a bit of history that didn't belong to these players. It took some time to grow our own history, and for people to believe in it. In that first derby, once again it was a new level. Their players were the icons of WA football – guys like McKenna, Mainwaring, Worsfold, Matera, Turley, Hart and Sumich. They had the class, and they were a much better team of individuals than us by a country mile; we were the new kids on the block. And they became our natural enemy right away, because it wasn't a one-team town anymore. They came out in the press with Mick Malthouse's classic, "Oh, it's just another game," and they didn't really acknowledge us, but behind closed doors they were intent on showing everyone that they were the powerhouse of WA footy, they certainly came out and did that. Some of their players had career-best games. And it was the build-up to the game that for us created the rivalry straight away. I sensed that we could lift, because you're always trying to prove yourself as a footy player, and as a person.'

Shaun was also there for Fremantle's first derby win, after some five years of trying. 'When we won that first derby it was like we won the grand final. We were all in the moment, and it felt like we were a better team, we were never going to lose that game. None of their names mattered, and none of their performances. Mentally, we were up for it, and we wondered why we couldn't do that all the time. It was a massive celebration afterwards, we all ended up at the Left Bank and it was going off, it was going bananas. People doing laps around Fremantle in their cars, waving flags, it was absolutely fantastic. If anything, I was a little embarrassed by it, because you should always be able to beat another team, no matter who they are. I guess it was more about the journey, and where we were on that journey. The following day the derby win was on the front page of *The Australian* – with Brad Wira and myself slapping a high five.'

McManus played through the difficult years, but also during that transitional period when the Dockers came to dominate the Eagles, regardless of their respective ladder positions. 'We generally had no time for the Eagles, because they really rubbed our noses in it when they were victorious. They were taking out double-page ads in the papers, and slagging us off; I didn't think that was very gracious at all. I mean we had guys like Pav and McPharlin, Troy Cook, Peter Bell and the Carr brothers, who were always up for the derbies. There was one instance in a derby where there was a contested ball between Troy Cook and Mitchell White, and Cookie just smashed him. Cookie's the same size as me, and Mitchell White's like six foot four, but Cookie was just so hard at the ball and passionate about the club as well. The Carr brothers were fierce, and we were able to play against an Eagles midfield of Cousins, Judd, Kerr, Braun and Fletcher, because the guys I played with were mentally harder and up for that big game. We were sick of those guys prancing around town, and we knew what was going on behind the scenes with some of them, even if the West Coast Eagles had no idea about it, miraculously. We had plenty of mail on them, and we used that in the 2006 game. It was really led by Josh and Matty Carr – they had mates who'd given them the information, and so we got stuck into them with chirp on the field. It was great fun. We were never going to lose that game, and if we'd met them in the grand final we would have won that too – we had the wood on them big-time. I just felt comfortable that we could beat their midfield, and even though on paper they had a Brownlow Medallist, we had what I thought of as hardened warriors.'

Preparing for the derby games as a younger player meant listening to Metallica, and then later dance beats through headphones, but once Shaun became part of the leadership group he put on a brave face in the rooms before the game, and pretended to be calm. 'I'd just walk around telling gags and mucking around to calm my nerves, but inside I was deadly serious.' Like most professional athletes, Shaun relied on proper preparation rather than rituals or lucky charms to get himself ready, although he 'used to wear grey Bonds jocks a lot, and Pav used to wear red ones. The Carr brothers used to swap their jocks a lot because their mum would buy them a six-pack of jocks, and you know, sometimes they had those shitty mustard ones on.' Once on the field, however, the ritual was the same. 'After our warm-up I went around to all the guys, and gave them a hug to wish them good luck. Y'know, just a really good embrace that always ended with Pav, to reinforce that this really means something, and that we're going into battle.'

Shaun's last AFL game was a derby which, again, 'we were never going to lose, and I'll always feel proud of being able to wear my number 8 jumper for a final time, and walk through the tunnel, and of the guys who all played a great game. I'll always feel a debt to guys like David Mundy, and Luke McPharlin and Pav, for performing so well in my final game.'

It never eventuated, but had Fremantle played the Eagles in a derby grand final, Shaun would have wanted Matthew Pavlich to take the winning kick. 'I think of the journey he's been on with the club, and what a champion he's been, and if Pav had kicked the goal it would have been like destiny, there wouldn't be any doubt in my mind that the ball would go through. You'd be hard-pressed to stop me jumping the fence.'

Shaun has plenty of media commitments these days and an otherwise busy life, but although he retired in 2008 it doesn't feel that long ago. He still trains at East Fremantle oval a couple of days a week, and when running he visualises playing football and making the times he'd set himself during his career. Having pushed himself so hard for so many years to achieve at the AFL level, it's a difficult thing to let go of. He still thinks about the little things he could've done to improve his game, even though he 'couldn't have trained any harder.' Watching the derby games he 'rides every bump, and it's like I'm bleeding inside and I'm just praying to God that we win. When I get to a game I find it very hard to hold my tongue – I'm just immersed in it again. I'm a shithouse loser, and especially against West Coast. I absolutely ride every bump and I do take it personally. In my mind I'm still playing, and I feel like I could jump the fence and be part of it. I'm always going to be that guy.'

DENNIS LILLEE – EAGLES

Dennis Lillee looks relaxed and comfortable in jeans and a checked shirt, sleeves rolled up. He appears just as lithe as when he debuted for Western Australia in 1969/70 aged twenty, taking thirty-two wickets for the season and ending up WA's leading wicket-taker. The flowing '70s locks are gone, but the trademark mo remains in place. There's warmth and generosity in his eyes, as well, with just that hint of mischief that made him a favourite with cricket fans. A mischief that darkened when he took the new ball and turned to face the opening batsmen, becoming a predatory gleam because – more than any fast-bowler before or since – Dennis Keith Lillee had the action and the control and the pace (measured at 155kph in the mid-'70s) to terrorise with one ball and fatally tempt with the next. Caught Marsh, bowled Lillee (this happened ninety-five times), Thommo up one end and Lillee at the other, the WACA crowd chanting his name in the final session of the second Ashes test in 1974, as shadows played across the ground, the English batsmen visibly tormented – these were the iconic cricketing moments for a generation of West Australians.

Dennis Lillee grew up in East Belmont. His father had tried out for East Perth Football Club when he lived in the country, and so Dennis grew up supporting his dad's team, although his mother followed West Perth because of her own familial loyalty (her great-grandfather Jack Kneale had been a founding member of the club back in 1885). Dennis grew up watching East Perth games with his brother, especially sitting 'on Chaddy's wing the whole time. When they turned around and went the other way, we went on the other wing, and then we went around the other one, so yeah we were fanatical.' When asked to name his favourite player from the period, he jokes, 'Do you want me to name the whole team?' Then he manages to name most of them: Square Kilmurray, Derek Chadwick, Paul Seal, Polly Farmer, Neil Hawke, Dobbie Graham, Keithy Doncon, Ken McAullay and others.

Dennis was a skilled player in both cricket and footy, and so didn't have to make the choice between the sports until relatively late. 'In those days you didn't have to make a decision because each of the seasons didn't really cross over. So, for example, Ken McAullay and Derek Chadwick played both sports. And they played both sports for WA. So you could get away with it, but it was getting harder. I was playing under-eighteens football and playing A-grade cricket for Perth Cricket Club when I was sixteen, so I guess at that stage I was starting to think that cricket was probably the way to go. The decision was due to the fact that I was playing first-grade cricket but I could still play football. I could have gone down to the Swans, but the turning point was when one day I went for a mark at full forward and landed right on my coccyx, and I was out for a while. I think that injury gave me a little bit of time out of the start of the cricket season, and I think because I started to play A-grade at sixteen probably tipped the scales a bit. And funnily enough, I thought, "This is a bit *dangerous*," and I started to worry a bit. Because it really did cause some concern, and ironically I went and played cricket and ended up having three stress fractures in my back, which is nothing to do with the other thing, but it's funny how you worry about one thing yet, you know, I played the other sport and the worst thing that could possibly happen, happened in the other sport.'

Famously, as a result of the injury, Dennis spent six weeks in a full-torso cast and then a couple of months in a torso-brace, until a training regime instituted by Dr Frank Pyke brought him back to play again after nearly two years out of the game (the fact that he still trains five or six days a week is a product of its effectiveness).

Touring with the Australian side, particularly the Ashes tours during the British summer, presented difficulties when it came to keeping in touch with WAFL footy scores. 'It seems sort of like when the ark was launched now, when you think about the way we did it. We actively sought out the scores and we were in touch with the people who looked after us, and the people from the High Commission. So they'd have functions for the team and they'd come to the cricket, so that was one of the ways. You'd also have one or two of the reporters that were from Western Australia, or from a footy-playing state, and you hounded them to get the scores. We pleaded with them to give us a score as soon as they could get one, so that was how we kept up with our team's results. It was how we kept in touch, and it was on in the dressing-room because everyone barracked for different teams, and of course the blokes from New South Wales used to rubbish us and say, "Oh it's bloody aerial ping-pong," and we used to give them a go at what we thought their sport was.'

It was the traditional West Australian antipathy towards 'the Vics' that cemented Dennis's interest in the West Coast Eagles when the national competition was introduced. This had a lot to do with the intensity of the interstate footy games at a time when they meant something, but also the fact that Western Australia was the relative newcomer to the Sheffield Shield competition when Dennis began playing (the WA cricket team was only accepted as a full member of the Shield in 1947/48). There was a perceived arrogance born out of excellence that traditionally came from Victorian cricket teams, as the team with a longer history, and so the opportunity for a WA football team to play Victorian teams every week was enticing. Dennis and his extended family became Eagles fans on the back of this reality, and have remained so and, although he admits that the Eagles were a veritable state side playing Victorian club teams, he still 'lapped it up'. He became the Eagles number-one ticket holder for two years, and his early club favourites included Glen Jakovich, Ross Glendinning, Laurie Keene and guys like Guy McKenna 'who were hard workers that weren't necessarily what you would call stand-out naturals, but just were hardworking, methodical and reliable. You could see they'd be the last on the training track, and they were the sort of guys I admired, not the showy ones particularly.' This makes sense in the context of Dennis's own career, when he admits that he 'never enjoyed the adulation. But when I trained I had to do something extra each time, hoping that that might get me an extra wicket if I beat whatever I was trying to do. Every game was a grand final; that's how I played the game, where you never leave anything on the track.'

For the same reasons that he welcomed a West Australian team entering the national footy competition and taking it to the Vics, Dennis similarly thought the introduction of the Fremantle Dockers a good move, as a team that he has 'a soft spot for because I think they've done it harder than the Eagles initially. I just admire the way that they've progressed through getting rid of who they had to, whether it be playing staff or coaches, to get to where they've got to now. The Eagles were lucky that we had a great team to start with, and we were lucky enough as it turned out to have a great coach [in Malthouse]. But I see a confidence creeping into the Fremantle club and I like the way they play.'

However, Dennis is quick to add, laughing, 'The only time I haven't got a soft spot for the Dockers is when they're playing West Coast, and then I hate them like any Eagles fan. I just think that for the last ten years it's irked me that Freo have done so well against us. They seemed to have worked us out, and often we've had no answer to them, although West Coast are a far better side now and I always look forward to the derbies.'

The perfect scenario for Dennis, then, is a situation where both teams are performing well, although perhaps one less successfully than the other, leading to a derby grand final one day, which would really drive the Vics crazy. 'I won't call it, because it'd put the mockers on, but I wouldn't be at all surprised if it happens. And the thing is, how would they handle that in the Eastern States? How would the Vics take it and how many would turn up? It's an interesting question.'

In the meantime, Dennis is happy to transition into retirement, and suggests that this might be one of his last interviews. He's just returned from a trip around France with his wife, where he explored his passion for wine collecting and drinking a bit of course. The boxes of wine from the trip have arrived that morning. He jokes about a custom-designed wine rack that can protect his wine from the extremes of his next car trip to the Kimberley.

He has already begun pulling back from sponsorships and charity events, having put in some forty years of service to charitable organisations. He's moved away from his work with the MRF Pace Foundation in Chennai, India, and quit his longstanding role as president of the WACA. There is a poignancy in his honesty about his reasons for doing this. 'Three score and ten is what they say, isn't it? You know I've got four years left basically until then. I think it's time to do a bit for myself before the end. It comes with the territory, I know, but I never asked for the adulation and I don't enjoy it. I think it's just time for me to take a step back.'

MARIA GIGLIA – DOCKERS

The first time Maria Giglia's father and mother looked at her handiwork at a Dockers home game, they were shocked. Out there on Subiaco Oval the Freo players emerged to the usual roar of the crowd, and ran towards the crepe Dockers banner that Maria and her team had so lovingly created, but what happened next took them by surprise. With lives focused on hard work, they'd never taken much of an interest in footy until Maria took over making the Dockers home-game banners. Then they never missed a game, just so they could admire her team's handiwork in those clean magnificent seconds before it was torn apart. But on that first occasion they asked, 'You mean, they rip it? All that work you put into it, and they run through it and rip it?'

Maria Giglia is picking Italian parsley in the front yard of her Fremantle home when I arrive. It's a beautiful winter's afternoon and, inside, the smell of meatballs and sauce fills her kitchen. Above the kitchen table is a Dockers flag, and Maria takes a seat, cradling her painful knee. As a girl growing up in Lathlain in a strict Italian family, she wasn't allowed to play sport. Despite this, she played netball, although she always had to conceal her injuries from her father, and the consequences have been carried through her life. Another aspect of her upbringing was that she wasn't allowed to go to football games, and so only came to her love of the game once she'd started her own family. She was never particularly interested in the Eagles, but when the Dockers were inaugurated, and the offer of Harbour Master tickets was made to support the founding of the club, she thought first of her husband, 'who used to work seven days a week from six in the morning until nine at night.' She thought he deserved a break, and so bought him and his brother memberships, and season tickets for her two children. Maria adds with a laugh that the hope was also that while they were at the game, she might get some 'peace and quiet'. But to gauge how they'd be feeling upon their return, she began to listen to the games on her radio while she did housework, and she was hooked. When her children decided to join the cheer squad, and a seat became available, Maria went to her first Dockers game, and she's been going ever since.

During Fremantle's first season, rather than running through a banner, the team ran through a rather cheesy-looking inflatable shipping container. Apparently the players weren't too keen on the gimmick, and asked for a banner just like the other clubs. Initially, the home-ground banners were made in Victoria, by a keen group of new Dockers fans who'd previously supported Geelong (this rather incredible team of people still makes the away-game banners, including for games in NSW, Queensland and Tasmania). The banners were flown over to Perth for game day. This period ended when the banners began to be made locally, at the Fremantle Passenger Terminal. As a Harbour Master, Maria was invited to participate. By chance, on her first night, she drove her station wagon, and when the completed banner wasn't picked up she offered to deliver it to the club. This became the weekly practice and began a period where, for every logistical problem that developed (and there were many), Maria and her team became the solution. This ultimately meant making the banner at the John Curtin Senior High School gymnasium every Monday night, coming up with a banner 'saying', storing it throughout the week and then delivering it to the ground two hours before the start of play (where the banner poles were kept), 'poling it up' and then waiting for the team to run through it before packing it away.

Now that Fremantle's colours are 'man purple' and white (it used to be four colours, and a lot more complicated for the banner team), the banners are made of metre-width 'logs' of purple crepe, held together by 'oodles' of sticky tape. The banner is reinforced on both sides, and then the letters are cut and added and sticky-taped into place. The whole process takes a group of between ten and sixteen volunteers several hours, and is completed over two weeks if there aren't enough people on the first night. More recently, because of the introduction of compulsory advertising 'wings' stationed beside the on-field banner, the length of the banner has been shortened from twenty metres to fourteen metres, and the banner team are no longer allowed to come up with the weekly slogan, which instead arrives from head office. There are also strict rules about the use of the once-traditional strip colours (they're banned), as Maria and her team found out one afternoon when they placed a green star next to David Mundy's name. Despite all this, and the fact that no matter how strong they make the banner, or how much tape they use, a good strong gust of wind on game day will always destroy their work ('The wind is the devil'). Regardless, for Maria the banner team is 'like a family. It's just a beautiful atmosphere. We've been together for fifteen years and we carry on like a family – there's lots of banter and carryings on and we just love being together.'

Asked to name her favourite banner, Maria doesn't need to think for long, although it wasn't for a Dockers game. She received a call on a Thursday afternoon from someone at the Swan Districts Football Club, and the caller was very apologetic. After all, they needed a banner for the Saturday game and that's a lot of work to complete in two nights. The caller began to explain the situation, but Maria stopped her.

She understood, she said. Nobody would ask for such a thing if it weren't important, and this turned out to be true. One of the Swan's trainers, a man who'd been part of the club for some fifty years, was at death's door. They just wanted the banner to read FOR JACK. If any evidence were needed that football clubs are like families, Maria goes on to describe how they arrived at Bassendean Oval the following day, 'and they told me that Jack passed away that morning, but that they hadn't told anyone. So we put up the banner, and in front of the crowd they announced that Jack had passed away that morning. Well, there wasn't a dry eye. All the players were crying, you know, it was just so emotional. To me that is the most special banner I've ever made, because it had lots of meaning.'

Regardless of the outcome of the games, there's a real collegial atmosphere between the banner teams, to the extent that Maria's team often helps the teams from the non-Victorian interstate clubs to set up (Victorian clubs have their own people), particularly the sole lady from the Gold Coast team who comes over, because 'banners are about celebrating, and you're there to help one another because one day you could be over there wanting help.' Maria is generally quick to smile and has a ready laugh, although she becomes serious when she adds that 'it's only the opposition fans that ruin the celebration, on occasions.' In particular, Maria's firsthand experiences with some Eagles fans, which have turned her against the rival club, 'not the Eagles team.' She's been out there at Subiaco Oval setting up her banner when some Eagles women have deliberately walked across the banner, in high heels, or have walked through it. Some Eagles fans 'have been really nasty to us. Very nasty and they still are, which is the sad part because the nastiness is what I hate.' At just over five feet tall, and a nonna, Maria isn't the most physically imposing figure, and it's a mystery to her why some Eagles fans at the ground are so vicious. She's met 'some nice people, who've come up and talked to us,' but she's also been spat upon, and abused, and 'the *women*, the disgusting language coming from the women at us.' The situation became so bad at Eagles home games that Maria now needs a security guard to accompany her along the boundary line, as she returns the tattered banner and heads to her seat.

Despite this, the banner team feels 'lost' in the off-season, especially on Monday nights when they usually convene. Maria's husband makes it through the cricket season by taping the Dockers' winning games, and watches a 'medicinal' game a week, simulating a winning season.

Maria's maternal instincts decide her favourite players, such as Brodie Holland, and all those seventeen- and eighteen-year-old players 'barely out of nappies' drafted from interstate, who're set up with Dockers foster-mums, and thereby become part of the Dockers family, until they 'know how to look after themselves.' Otherwise, her favourite long-term players are the captains, namely Peter Bell, who's 'such a lovely gentleman with a great sense of humour,' and Matthew Pavlich, 'who's just been so wonderful. He's such a gentleman.' Both captains were effective leaders because they're role models, and have looked after their younger team mates, and it's the same sense of caring that underwrites Maria's long-term support for the Dockers, especially in those early years when they were perennial underdogs. 'I've been to a game where there were only thirteen thousand people, and I always hoped that we'd win a premiership while Pavlich was captain, because he deserved it.' It's at this point that Maria introduces me to her grandson. Maria takes him onto her lap, and takes his hands. 'We clap for the Dockers, clap for the Dockers,' she sings, and the boy breaks into a big smile.

GILLIAN O'SHAUGHNESSY – DOCKERS

Gillian O'Shaughnessy looks remarkably lively when we meet her at the ABC studios in East Perth, considering she's just finished the early morning shift. The shift runs from four am through to ten, but means getting up at three every morning and going to bed at six. 'Gillo', as she's known to ABC 720 listeners, is one of Perth's best-known radio presenters, participating yearly at the Perth Writers Festival by way of her on-air book club. As a journalist with some twenty years experience, the temporary change of shift doesn't appear to faze her, despite it being extended for another short period. In the open-plan office on the other side of the glass panelling, the work of ABC programming continues in the background; there is the regular tapping of keyboards and an atmosphere of quiet anxiety as deadlines come and go, but in the meeting room where we're seated, Gill is beaming. After years of driving an old rust-bucket that needed hotwiring to spark the ignition, Gill has recently bought an olive Mini Cooper that she's named Clive, in honour of her all-time favourite Dockers player, Clive Waterhouse. For Gill, and for many Dockers fans, Waterhouse was a touchstone for the distinctive character of the club during those hard years when success was a distant dream. While getting pantsed on a weekly basis was the reality, Waterhouse's mercurial talent and capacity for slapstick error provided light relief, as well as a window into a time when rare moments of brilliance might be translated into regular success. This is the poetry of the underdog, made flesh-and-blood in the form of a blond-haired enigma who'd regularly bomb a goal from a fifty-metre flank but miss from directly in front.

Gill is a Freo person through and through, and her deep love of the Dockers stems from a deep love of Fremantle itself. She grew up in Bunbury, but 'moved to Cottesloe after her parents' divorce, living with her hippy mother.' The experience was one of dislocation, however, because Gill didn't share the privilege of many of her school friends, something exemplified in the image of Gill's only toy – a one-armed Barbie doll. It was only when Gill's 'family moved to Fremantle that she felt truly at home, among the other misfits, children of migrants, hippies and oddballs,' solidifying her respect for and understanding of the outsider. Gill attended first South Fremantle Senior High and later John Curtin Senior High School, and it was during this period that she began, like many of her friends, to wear a long South Fremantle Bulldogs scarf, draping herself with the red and the white. Following the game of football then had everything to do with the social aspect of sitting with her friends at Fremantle Oval, watching the Doggies train and play on the weekends.

Being a Freo person, Gillian O'Shaughnessy was always going to wait patiently for her beloved port city to field its own team. She was never going to follow the Eagles, a 'team without a fixed geographical identity that instead claimed the whole state as its own.' Perhaps this failure to develop any love for the first WA AFL franchise was cemented by one of her first assignments as a journalist when, in the late '90s, she was sent by an unforgiving superior to elicit from the famously cranky Eagles coach, Mick Malthouse, confirmation of club legend Chris Mainwaring's rumoured retirement. Terrified of the fierce leader and her fiercer sub-editor, Gill nevertheless persisted, 'and after much anxiety was finally rewarded with a curt nod.'

This of course was around the time of the Dockers' first derby win, after failing at nine previous attempts. The Dockers of 1999 who triumphed in that first derby also had another drawcard for Gill – namely 'Tony Modra's biceps', which were put into good use in his now-famous ground-slapping celebration after snapping the goal that sealed the win. Invited to watch a game with friends in Telstra's corporate box, Gill apparently was overwhelmed at the sight of the devilishly handsome Modra and shouted out, 'Kick it nude!' She was never invited back.

This passion for the team and outspokenness means that Gill prefers to watch the game at home, with her patient husband and one trusted friend. She'd never consider watching a derby game with an Eagles fan in the room, but has a Collingwood supporting friend who she makes an exception for. Another outsider. Wearing her 'lucky Dockers scarf, the television set and record player draped with another four lucky scarves, and purple flowers set around the room' to complete the voodoo harmony necessary to get her team over the line, when the game runs counter to expectations, Gill's not above shifting her viewing position to realign the psychic balance and 'shift the flow and increase the luck.' Seated in the now correct position, and with her husband Glynn sometimes standing next to the couch like an aerial channelling the kind of Jedi energy necessary to get their team a win, Gill is free to 'shout and curse' as much as she likes, although she 'never criticises Freo, not the players, certainly not the coach.'

You can tell that Gill is the kind of fan 'who can't stand fence-sitters', that is, those Eagles supporters who name Freo as their second team. Such a hardline position is easy to maintain for your average punter, but complicated when you're a public personality in dialogue with a radio audience made up of fans from both clubs, working alongside colleagues who also support West Coast. There was a brief time at ABC 720 when the Dockers had the trifecta – Geoff Hutchison on *Mornings*, Gill on *Afternoons* and John McGlue on *Drive* – but it hasn't always been that way. Russell Woolf was always good for 'an anti-Dockers gibe, happy to give as good as he got.' According to Gill their regular pre-game banter and bet of a cheese-wheel on the derby games was one of her favourite things about footy. Especially as, at last count, she was well ahead. And Gill is not only prepared to put her money where her mouth is. She once wagered the outcome of a derby game with her Friday regular sport commentator in what must be the ultimate bet. Each was asked to name their worst fear. Gill's was 'a fear of heights, and Lachy Reid's was a terrible fear of snakes' – both well recognised phobias that have the capacity to paralyse a sufferer with dread. Gill reluctantly agreed 'to parachute-jump out of an aeroplane' if she lost the bet, and Lachy 'offered to handle a snake on live radio.' Fortunately for Gill, the Dockers prevailed on that occasion, and her colleague was forced to endure the 'wearing of a python around his neck in the studio.' It was a good bet to win, and a bad bet to lose.

It's often been said that living in Fremantle can be like living in a bubble. A bubble, or an ark of like-minded souls who follow the one football team and drink good coffee. But Gill is the first to admit that while her job at ABC 720 hasn't led to a diminishment of her disdain for the Eagles, particularly come derby day; she is however open to admitting that she's met plenty of Eagles fans 'who appear normal enough.' One example was when Gill was required by her boss to wear an Eagles scarf in Fed Square in Melbourne during a live broadcast before the 2015 grand final, interviewing fans on their way to see the Eagles humiliated by Hawthorn, as Fremantle had been a couple of years previously. She chatted with fans, developed 'an unexpected but welcome attachment to Sam Butler's mum and enjoyed the festive air and the live soundtrack provided by Five Seconds of Summer and their large throng of teenage followers', although 'it was the sight of Matthew Pavlich walking across the other side of Fed Square' (her post-Clive, post-Modra favourite player, along with Hayden Ballantyne) that made the day. On air, Gill was so overcome at spotting her captain, she shrieked live to air and off script, 'It's Pav, it's Pav!' before remembering herself and the sensitivities involved. 'For his part, Pav, clearly wary of the likelihood of being accosted by the overzealous and the shrill on grand final weekend, visibly jumped, fixed his gaze to the front, and notably increased his pace in the opposite direction, close to, but not quite breaking into, a run.' And this was not the first occasion this had happened. Twice before, when the Dockers captain visited the studio to be interviewed by another presenter, Gill was immediately alerted by colleagues who pointed him out, urging her to present herself to her hero. She 'demurred, wanting to preserve what was left of her dignity, and mortified at the sight of an increasingly alarmed Pavlich who could not take three steps through the ABC headquarters without yet another well-meaning person tapping him on the arm and helpfully pointing out his greatest fan cringing in the studio.' Like most Dockers fans, Gill agrees that it's a tragedy that Matthew Pavlich retired without holding aloft the premiership cup, and not only because he stuck with the club through its darkest times, but also because he played in the same forward line as Clive Waterhouse, and emerged unscathed. As a man of dignity he carried the disappointment of the 2013 loss, and he undoubtedly deserved the ultimate win.

MATT QUINN AKA MR Q – EAGLES

With his nightclub tan and quiet, self-deprecating demeanour, Matt Quinn looks every bit the behind-the-scenes computer guy behind the mysterious avatar, Mr Q. We meet for a pint in a northern-suburbs pub, and take a quiet and darkened corner. He's the founder and administrator of the Eagles' main fan website *EaglesFlyingHigh*, whose role is building content and monitoring an overloaded message board at all hours of day and night. Although the site is invigilated by a couple of others with administrative privileges, it's a significant amount of work running a fan website for a club with a membership north of fifty thousand, and footy fans can be passionate, perverse, hypersensitive and belligerent, sometimes in the one post. And yet Matt is not only happily married, but also manages to hold down a full-time job in Curtin's Technology Park at Bentley.

EaglesFlyingHigh is a virtual community whose black box is Matt's computer in the back room of his house. He started it as a 'little blog thing' back in 2003, then added a message board, and 'like all message boards it took over as the main event.' Because every football club these days employs a media department to control the spin, a place where fans come together to share stories and hatreds and opinions, and feel like they're part of the bigger picture was always going to be popular. Matt's job is to monitor the behaviour of the posters and warn or delete those people who stray into defamatory abuse or unnecessary criticism of players or other fans. As with all footy websites, a bad game from the team can draw out people who are emotional and looking for someone to blame. While most regular posters employ a deal of wit and so can be trusted, Matt's work doesn't end there – game previews and game round-ups need to be written. This all adds up to a lot of time spent in his back room.

Matt's family are fifth-generation West Australians. The Quinns originally came out, like so many Victorians, to escape the Depression and seek their fortune in the Goldfields. This they 'did by catering to miners' needs – some Quinns were tailors and another ran a pub in North Fremantle.' Matt's father played footy for East Perth in the reserves, and his uncle played in the firsts, but 'unfortunately those sports genes didn't follow down to me, although I played a few years at the end of high school at Aquinas. About the only thing I liked doing at Aquinas was the footy. I enjoyed getting out there in the thirds but I knew at the end where my footy career was going and that was absolutely nowhere.' There's a hint of regret in Matt's matter-of-fact recognition of his lack of sporting talent, although he describes with a laugh how he 'once took a screamer of a mark over [later Dockers legend] Stephen O'Reilly. He was on my team unfortunately, and I think it was more of an accident than anything else. He stumbled running at the ball and I was running in from behind him and as he stood up he lifted me in the air and the ball landed in my hands and I looked down and thought, "*Holy shit,* this guy is tall." Everyone who saw it was laughing because nobody could imagine me taking a speccy, but I managed to get the ball onto one of my team mates so that was alright.'

When the Quinn family moved to Floreat Park, Matt's father and brothers defected from following East Perth and took up with Claremont, although Matt kept with East Perth, a decision he's been paying for over the years, 'especially in the 1996 WAFL grand final when Claremont got the last goal of the match to win by two points.' Nevertheless, the Quinns often went to WAFL games together, although Matt confesses that it was often the bribery factor of Choc 99s that got him there.

Matt was an eighteen-year-old uni student when the Eagles came along. At that time it was both cheap and possible to turn up at an Eagles home game and buy a ticket on the gate. He went whenever he could, along with a friend who later defected to become a Dockers fan (he doesn't hold it against him, because his friend did it at the beginning of the Dockers' first season – Matt's disdain is reserved for those who jumped ship when the Dockers started having some success). Either way, it was the experience of going to live games that captured Matt's attention, and made him the passionate fan he is today. In particular, one game against Collingwood – where the ground was packed and the atmosphere was intense, and the Eagles won the game and the crowd went wild – got Matt hooked. There was also a level of professionalism displayed by the Eagles that was new and exciting, and the team of '91 was a stand-out (he still hasn't forgiven his uni lecturer who wouldn't let him go to the '92 grand final). Matt makes the valid point that the Eagles have been around for thirty years now, which isn't an insignificant amount of time for a club to develop a culture and a history – in that 'anyone younger than thirty won't remember a time when Perth didn't have an AFL club, even if in Victoria others might regard that history as unimportant in the context of the longer VFL club histories.' Matt has been a member since the Eagles' early days, and has seats alongside his mother and father, and he's been going to home games for all of his adult life.

He wasn't annoyed, like some others, when the Fremantle Dockers entered the competition, believing that Perth deserved a second team, especially when he went to the first derby, thereafter known to Eagles fans as the Mother's Day Massacre (Freo lost by 85 points.) It was hard to hate the Dockers when they were merely 'whipping boys, and gave up the four points with little fuss, allowing the Eagles to focus on the big picture.' Comical, too, according to Matt, was how the Dockers used to make a big occasion of the derbies, mainly because they weren't in the picture for the grand prize. This was illustrated for Matt during the 2006 season, when Freo won both derbies but the Eagles won the flag. Clearly, the Dockers of yore had their priorities back to front. Saying that, he adds now that both teams are more evenly matched, the derby is 'a serious rivalry, and its divisive and tribal aspects make the lead-ups to derby week more lively than they once were.'

While 'there have been some terrific contests over the years,' of all the derbies it's Fremantle's first win in 1999 that sticks in his mind, the Dockers having lost the first nine. This has something to do with 'the shock of that first loss, and a dawning awareness that Fremantle might be on the rise' (this turned out to be a false dawn for Fremantle, who lost their next seven games, including all six remaining matches of 1999), but also the sense of nostalgia associated with the loss, spelling out the end of a 'golden era' for the Eagles, when 'you could sense that time was up on that great team and players like Jakovich and McIntosh and others.'

One of the best recent derby wins was the second derby of 2015. And credit where it's due, he says, 'Fremantle were an outstanding team that year. But for the second derby, it showed the Eagles as a team that a lot of people had underrated – beating the top team – and that was the best that the Eagles could have played with an undermanned team. They took their opportunity and in a lot of ways it propelled them into the grand final where unfortunately they forgot to turn up and were overawed by the occasion as

Fremantle had been overawed in 2013.'

In the meantime, there are future seasons to look forward to, and the experience of going to every home game and sitting with his family, and the familiar faces around them and 'knowing everyone and saying hi to everyone and talking to the people around us.' This is the physical manifestation of a virtual community that he participates in nightly on the *EaglesFlyingHigh* website, although both are 'a dedicated, dedicated group of Eagles fans.' Some Dockers fans are regulars on the message boards, although there aren't many, and there's little to no contact between *EaglesFlyingHigh* and *Dockerland*. In 2006, he tried to goad the *Dockerland* administrator into a bet where in the event of a derby grand final, *EaglesFlyingHigh* would fly the Dockers colours if the Eagles lost, and *Dockerland* would be rebranded *Eagleland* in the event of a win, but his postings kept getting deleted before they could be read, and in any event the challenge became unnecessary when the Eagles fronted the Swans in the GF.

By temperament, Matt's not a hater, which is just as well, and something of a dreamer, literally. He describes a recent dream in which he 'was actually a good footballer, and I was playing for the Eagles, and I was playing forward, and I even managed to mark the ball, which is something that I couldn't actually do when I was playing the game.' Matt's wife is a Freo fan, which isn't as complicated as it sounds, he assures me, although he's constantly being reminded that not everybody is so moderate in their views. Saying that, it was both a bit awkward and a little unfair at his wedding, when his brother made a speech about welcoming a Dockers fan into the Quinn family, which 'was a real no-no,' although his comment got a few laughs. But the DJ must have picked up on it, 'because minutes later he spun the Dockers club song on the turntable,' the memory of which brings a wry smile to Matt's face.

FEDELE CAMARDA – DOCKERS

We plan to meet Fedele in the old grandstand at Fremantle Oval, but get there to find a maintenance bloke wandering about bashing the old jarrah plank seats into place with a mallet. Instead, Dockers media guy Luke Morfesse finds us a place inside the nearby Dockers clubhouse. The good news is that we're allowed to use the media room and, in his Dockers team shirt, Fedele Camarda looks every bit the sportsman seated in front of the sponsors' wallpaper screen used in Dockers media conferences. In his forties now, and the father of three boys, Fedele still plays competition sport and maintains an active role in his children's clubs. He grew up in Fremantle, and played some colts football for Souths, but Fedele is also a third-generation lobster fisherman working out of Fremantle and the demands of work often clashed with his football. He grew up playing alongside Scott Watters and Peter Sumich and against John Worsfold, before captaining the Cockburn team that he played with in the Peel Football League, until his late twenties.

Fedele suggested the old grandstand as a place to meet because of the memories associated with being a Freo boy supporting Souths, and walking up from his grandfather's house on Norfolk Street with his brothers and sister to watch the game with his father and his mates. As a child, Fedele was lucky enough to watch the likes of Stephen Michael, Maurice Rioli, Rod Barrett and Benny Vigona and 'that's what really got me into watching footy. Souths didn't win the flags you might have hoped for, but the football was so exciting, and the skills were so good, that I still think it was the best footy ever. These days the coaches are too good at what they do, and have too much influence. In those days players played positions, and so there were more one-on-ones, they didn't rotate guys off the boundary like they do today.'

Fedele's grandfather migrated to Western Australia early in the 1900s, aged twelve, but after a short stint back in his native Sicily, he returned to Fremantle and was one of the pioneers of the crayfishing industry. Fedele's father was one of nine children who grew up on Norfolk Street in Fremantle, half of whom barracked for South Fremantle and half for East Fremantle (both teams were based at Fremantle Oval at that time). Fedele's grandfather was an Old Easts man, but like his father, Fedele and all of his brothers and sister followed the Bulldogs. The port team rivalries were fierce in those days and the fact that many of Fedele's uncles and cousins supported East Fremantle made for a lively atmosphere. He remembers how, after the 1979 derby grand final (which featured the biggest ever crowd at Subiaco Oval) with East Fremantle winning, there was a family wedding the same evening. What he remembers most about the wedding is that one of his uncles wore a blue and white beanie – 'more memorable than the fact that Jackie Love was the entertainment.'

When the Eagles emerged as West Australia's first AFL team, Fedele wasn't lured into following them. Like many others, Fedele 'loved the WAFL, because I love Fremantle and I'm proud of where I come from. I loved the tribalism associated with identifying with a geographical place, and the Eagles seemed like an "entity" rather than a club. They were listed on the stock exchange, and I didn't see it as a football club. And their supporters didn't seem like traditional football supporters. I'm generalising, but they seemed like the kind of people who jumped on the Perth Wildcats bandwagon during the '80s when they were having a good run. Armchair supporters. The chardonnay set. Whereas we used to go to all the WAFL games, win or lose, home and away. We used to go to all the grounds by train when we were old enough. There was already talk about a Fremantle AFL team and we decided to wait for that. Something not advertised nearly enough,' he continues, 'is how entrenched the football culture is in Fremantle, and how proud we are of it. We've had two teams in the WAFL since 1900 and between them and the original Fremantle they've won nearly half of all premierships. Everyone talks about the 1979 derby grand final as being one of the pinnacles of football in this state. And later, half of the premiership-winning Eagles team players were from either South or East Fremantle.'

But not all of Fedele's family and friends held the course and waited for the Dockers. He estimates that there are about 'thirty per cent' who're Eagles supporters, and that fraction is enough to create friction. Like many Dockers supporters, one thing that's confirmed Fedele in his support for the AFL port team over the years is the merciless and 'irrational' ribbing he's endured. Some of it is good-humoured, fortunately, but some of it is 'arrogant and feral – mainly from people who can't stand the thought of Fremantle having any success.' He works alongside an Eagles-supporting cousin on the cray-boat who has a soft spot for the Dockers having grown up in Freo himself. One longstanding tradition is that during the Blessing of the Fleet in Fremantle, when a statue of the Madonna is carried through the streets to bring good luck and protection to the port city's fishermen, in a ceremony that dates back to 1948, Fedele makes sure that their parade boat always flies the Dockers and the South Fremantle flag. 'You've got all the religious festivities going on but it adds to the occasion to have that Dockers flag up there with the South Fremantle flag.' This is, of course, because some of the other fishing boats fly the Eagles flag, and there's always 'competition to see whose flag can be raised highest.'

Something else Fedele is justifiably proud of as a Freo punter, was the result of a chance meeting on the train after a home game when the Dockers had been thrashed. He got into 'a passionate conversation' with another Dockers supporter, the 'impressive' Russell Collett. 'We were talking about what we could do to have an influence on the club's direction as supporters, and we swapped numbers and later, we got a group of people together and that's how the Freo Mob was born. Initially we were branded troublemakers and complainers, but the Freo Mob's ultimate objective was to get the club licence back from the WAFC, and have a separate club and not actually be WAFC brand B. We also wanted the board to be elected by club members.' They were stymied at every turn by Dockers CEO Cameron Schwab, and attacked by various members of the media. Initially George Grljusich was sceptical but after talking it out with Fedele and Russell it turned out their grievances and objectives were the same and in the best interests of Fremantle. Grljusich became a supporter of their cause, which eventually led to two positions on the board being member-elected, 'which we thought was a pretty good achievement, starting from nothing, but we'd still love to see the licence hanging on the wall in Freo.'

In the Camarda family, every derby game is eagerly awaited. Fedele was present at the very first derby back in 1995, and remembers the anticipation (having beaten Essendon the week before) as his team ran out onto the ground. The loss was terrible, although 'guys like Winston Abraham were doing some exciting things'. Later, Fremantle's first derby win was a major turning point and the Demolition Derby of 2000 was a 'real statement'. His favourite derby player over the years is Shaun McManus, who you could tell 'really loved Freo, and has a strong connection to Freo.' McManus famously suffered two serious knee injuries, and displayed a 'lot of courage to come back from that. He always put his body on the line and played two-hundred-odd games despite those injuries. You could never doubt his courage or his commitment. He was someone who played for the colours.' His recent favourites include Nat Fyfe for the same reason, and 'Mickey Walters who is probably my favourite player. He's a natural footballer, and probably the only forward in the league who plays with instinct. If he can kick a goal he'll have a go. Whereas for a lot of the time, a lot of the other players' football has become very robotic, and instead of having a shot they'll over-think it, and try to set someone up thirty out and in the corridor. But Walters isn't like that, and Stephen Hill is also a natural footballer, as is Connor Blakely, who moves well and kicks beautifully with both feet.'

Derby day rituals are confined to a few strict sets of behaviour. Firstly, 'always wearing the colours', no matter where he finds himself, and always taking 'his seat before the game starts and never moving while the play is on.' When an opposition player is kicking for goal, it's important to use the word 'MALOCCHIO!' (Italian for evil eye), and which is well-known to put the mocker on. This curse is something that Fedele grew up doing, along with the traditional 'PSSSSS!' at the opposition for the same reason, and which is still employed to good effect. Such things are needed, he feels, because of Fremantle's traditional suffering at the hands of ludicrously bad umpiring, regular uneven free-kick counts, and a terrible record at the tribunal. Sometimes it feels like Fremantle, according to one of Fedele's good friends, is the 'AFL's voodoo doll', and it's only reasonable therefore that every measure is used to even up the score.

The ultimate victory, however, would be to beat the Eagles in a grand final derby. 'I try to be humble in defeat,' Fedele says finally, 'and it doesn't matter to me that I might have to wait for success. You have to stick by your colours. But if we ever win a grand final, they are going to cop it.' He laughs. 'Those condescending, fence-sitting frontrunners will be running for cover!'

KIM SCOTT – DOCKERS

Western Australian of the Year. Twice winner of the Miles Franklin Literary Award and the WA Premier's Book Awards. Winner of the Australian Literary Society Gold Medal. Professor of Writing at Curtin University. One of Australia's most celebrated writers.

These are just some of the achievements on Kim Scott's resumé that might have included WAFL football player if not for a serious knee injury when Kim was a sixteen-year-old. He didn't grow up in a footy-mad environment, because there were 'probably no males in the household, now that I think about it. I had a dad but he wasn't always around.' There was kick-to-kick at Albany's Mount Lockyer Primary School, and no doubt the footy was booted around in the nearby streets where cousins and friends introduced him to the winter game, but it wasn't until he was in grade five or six that he really began to enjoy footy and 'leapt at it with enthusiasm.' He went to the same primary school as future Labor premier Alan Carpenter, who was then captain of the cricket and footy teams and, it seemed, everything else. Kim remembers his first game of cricket, taking the crease and facing up to his first ball and not really knowing how to hold the bat, and Alan Carpenter, 'who probably kept one end up for the whole innings' looking down the pitch at Kim and the bemused expression on his face. But it was the experience of Kim's first live footy match and seeing Noongar player Stan Loo playing in a grand final 'in the back pocket, taking screamers one after the other' that really captured his imagination.

Kim played footy during his teenage years for North Albany, Royals and Railways teams, and made the Great Southern squad for Country Week, where he was selected to play alongside another Noongar rover, Jimmy Krakouer. But this was also the week that Kim injured his knee. Kim was invited up by Claremont Football Club to train and see their knee specialist, but to no avail. A serious knee injury at the age of sixteen was a cruel blow, especially when plenty of Kim's peers started playing league for Claremont. He understandably lost interest in the game, because 'it was hurtful beyond the physical injury.'

Kim's great heroes were players like Barry Cable and Polly Farmer, who he remembers being carried off the field after winning a grand final for West Perth as captain/coach, and the thrill of getting near the great man. He continued to watch some of the WAFL and VFL games that involved players like the Krakouer brothers who he'd played against in his teens, but after training as a teacher and being posted to a remote school, and with a young family of his own, other interests took over – something that readers of Kim's three novels will no doubt be grateful for. Kim began his career as a writer and, between that and his teaching career, his interest in the footy tapered off.

A move back to his home base in Fremantle, and his two sons' developing curiosity about football saw a rekindling of Kim's interest in the winter game. The West Coast Eagles were brought into being, although the club name didn't appeal to him because it sounded like 'a grid iron team', to the point where 'all the marketing hype around it put me off.' Kim fondly remembers Alan Carpenter, then a television journalist, on the eve before West Coast played their first grand final, at the end of that night's *7.30 Report*, unbuttoning his shirt on camera and revealing a Geelong Cats guernsey underneath. 'I remember seeing that and thinking, "Oh, that's a brave act." But it was a fantastic thing to do, he must've known he'd irk most of his viewers. I don't think he liked the hype surrounding the emergence of the Eagles either.'

When Fremantle emerged as the second WA AFL team, it was a different story. 'Despite the funny name, the Dockers somehow had a very local feel – the influence of what Neesham had done in the WAFL was part of that, with very local support. There was also a bit of anti-West Coast hype involved and maybe I found that attractive.' This difference in attitude was only confirmed during those difficult early years for the Dockers, who didn't beat the Eagles for their first four and a half seasons. 'With [West Coast] winning so much, you develop certain sentiments; a bitterness reinforced by their swag and strut and sense of privilege.' Fremantle, however, had players that were distinctive in character and style, something to do initially with the free-flowing brand of football initiated by Gerard Neesham, whom Kim admired 'because of what he'd achieved at Claremont. I really liked the game style they were running with and it seemed to be a WAFL-derived one. I remember as a kid playing a few games up here [on Perth ovals], how high the ball would bounce. It was like a different ball almost because the bounce was more random than on the damp grounds I was used to. [Neesham's] was a game style that seemed perfect for Perth's conditions, and I got parochial about things like that.' The run-and-carry style of play inaugurated by Neesham, which has become such a part of the modern game, also suited the game's Indigenous players. Some of Kim's early favourites included Scotty Chisholm, aka The Prince of Pockets, 'because of his particular way of moving and his gracefulness.' Stephen Koops, 'another with that distinctive way of moving,' and Clem Michael were two others, the latter of whom 'reminded me of Polly Farmer.'

Other players Kim admired were Adrian Fletcher, who didn't move so fast but did so well, and Spider Burton, who 'was an endearing sort and I liked the way he moved around the field.' There were 'noble types' like Shaun McManus, Ben Allan and Peter Mann, and later, players whose football was distinctive and who were derby standouts like Jeff Farmer and Clive Waterhouse. More recently, Kim particularly admires Michael Walters, 'who lacks speed but he's very fast in confined spaces. He has great balance and every time the ball's in front of him and his opponent, it's about how he uses his body. His peripheral vision is also fantastic.' Stephen Hill is another, 'because he's so obviously graceful in motion but also because he does a lot of work inside with his hands, moving the ball to space, tapping it around in packs – I think he's clever that way.'

The derby that stays with Kim most of all is that first victory in 1999, and the more recent derby where Hayden Ballantyne had a shot after the siren and missed, although he'd started celebrating in a moment of tragi-comic drama to the point that 'I really felt for the man. You can imagine the great glory you'd feel [if he'd goaled]'. Kim doesn't mind watching the Eagles play, if only because of his admiration for some of the players, and because more broadly he watches football to observe the way certain players ply their craft rather than for the overall result: 'I have players that I like to watch more than anything else, and unfortunately they sometimes play for the wrong team, that's all.' Kim mentions Michael Polanyi, a philosopher he encountered as an undergraduate whose ideas of 'tacit knowledge' and what occurs in 'skilful performance' helped him understand the uncanny ability of certain players to control the ball, and inhabit the flow of play, beyond natural talent and years of practice. 'I used to think that happens with football when you're in the zone. You look at players like Walters and how he will suddenly do the unaccountable, or how the ball becomes an extension of himself – call it a football zen thing.'

'In a moment of mad optimism,' in recent years Kim bought plane tickets early for himself, his wife and two sons to Melbourne to watch the year's grand final. But in the meantime, surprising perhaps for a novelist, it's not the broader plot points of the football season, or the sense that football is a morality play with its own heroes and villains that keeps his interest, but rather those moments of unaccountable grace under fire, and passages of play that verge on the sublime that demand his attention – harking back to his first childhood experience in 1960s Albany of watching Stan Loo 'taking screamers one after the other from the back pocket.'

ROSS McLEAN – DOCKERS

When asked about his favourite derby result, Ross McLean pauses while a truck passes the outdoor pub bench where we're seated, down in the West End of Fremantle, just a few metres from the New Edition bookshop run by his son-in-law, Alan (an Eagles supporter), and daughter. Behind us, the pub is flying Dockers colours, and so are many of the shopfronts up and down the street. Ross was the Dockers chairman from 1999 to 2001, and he's invested in derby results beyond the normal passion. The Dockers of the late 1990s were struggling financially, as well as on the scoreboard. 'Oh, the first derby is my favourite win. We'd been beaten nine derby games in a row, and many of those were thrashings. We were regarded as the poor kids on the block because of the way we were born, without resources, without the sort of player concessions that other clubs had. We had a difficult birth, and the Eagles on the other hand were successful, and they were rich. Our supporters and their supporters were at odds; there was quite a lot of animosity and there was even some animosity between the playing groups. The Eagles hadn't exactly been generous in victory, and some of their players had shown a pretty conspicuous disrespect. That's why that first derby win was so important. It was almost like an obsession with our people, and so it was important to get the monkey off the back.'

Ross sighs and smiles, reliving the pleasure, anxiety and relief of that day in 1999. 'When we were in the rooms after the game, I asked Damian Drum [the coach] if I could address the players. It's the only time I've done it, and he said sure. It was an Eagles home game, and all I said to them was, "Thank you, on behalf of all the supporters who couldn't be here. We recognise this as an important moment for our club – our coming of age in WA, but also it's an important building block in the history of our club." That's what it felt like at the time, and that's why that game for me is the best derby. That evening in the South Fremantle Football clubrooms there must have been a couple of thousand people there – it was packed to the rafters, and the joy and jubilation was incredible. You had to be there to understand what that win meant to those people.'

Another truck passes, and Ross looks pensive. 'Unfortunately, we didn't win another game for the rest of the year. We lost the next six games. It was the sad irony of that victory that we thought we'd climbed Everest, but actually we'd just reached the base camp.'

Ross was born in the mid-1940s in Mt Lawley, and grew up in a very keen football family, as a third-generation East Perth supporter. He went to every game that East Perth played in the WAFL. Back then, in what must've been good training for those gruelling early Dockers years, 'Mick Cronin was the coach, and we just loved going there, even though we got flogged every week. Particularly when we came to Fremantle. Bernie Naylor would kick twenty goals and we'd lose by twenty-five.'

Like many WAFL fans, despite his team's on-field struggles, Ross's memory of the league is matter-of-fact. 'It was just part of growing up – seeing East Perth play. They were tough times, but the public could go and listen to the half-time address, and the players would be sitting around having a smoke listening to the coach. They were all amateur footballers. They weren't paid much and they had other jobs. But there was something about the club nature of the WAFL, and the suburban nature of the league, and the rivalries that existed that made it special to us – we knew the name of every player of every team in the competition. During the games one side was always unhappy with the umpire, and so there was always noise and booing. I remember Polly Farmer coming to the club and Ted Kilmurray and Jack Hunt. Jack Sheedy came to be our coach and we won some premierships. I mean, my father would turn in his grave to learn that Perth Oval is now a soccer ground.'

Ross's twin brother played some league games for East Perth but Ross focused on his studies, playing amateurs for the '60s UWA team that won the national varsity football competition and went through the season unbeaten, and later became known as The Invincibles. He entered politics, and was successful in winning the seat of Perth for the Liberal Party, serving in the House of Representatives from 1975 to 1983. During this time, and busy with family (he has five children) and travelling to Canberra, he maintained his following of East Perth but wasn't too interested in the VFL: 'I didn't have a lot of time – being in a marginal seat and having to go to Canberra during the week, and returning home on the weekends – it was family, and it was work.'

When the Eagles entered the competition in 1987, Ross and his family became fans. 'Everyone wanted to be part of it – it was like having a state team. We took our kids to the games and got behind them even though I still barracked for East Perth.' The new AFL franchise had early success, although there's ambivalence in Ross's description of those early years because of the effect this had on the WAFL. 'I went to the Eagles' first game, and it was immediately followed by a WAFL game, and there was no interest in that WAFL game. There was an immediate impact, and the WAFL became a kind of secondary competition, which was sudden and sad. It's become even sadder in my view because the WAFL clubs run on the smell of an oily rag – they run chook raffles, they have volunteer staff, and compare that with the hubris and extravagance of the AFL. There's very little flowing down to the WAFL clubs.'

Ross followed the Eagles but felt a growing unease, having supported a WAFL club with a strong sense of local identity. 'The Eagles – it wasn't the Perth team. It didn't have a geographical identity. There's a good point that Dennis Cometti made a few years back – that it's a pity that the Eagles were named "West Coast", and instead they should have been called Perth. And we also detected a certain amount of arrogance about the club – a disconnect between the supporters and the club itself, which felt more like a professional business than a football family.'

Despite the Dockers coming into the competition, and in spite of his growing ambivalence, Ross continued to support the Eagles. And yet he was beguiled by certain aspects of the port club. 'When Fremantle came along they had an interesting coach who actually changed the way that football was played. [Gerard Neesham] played a possession game, holding onto the ball longer and drawing a player then freeing up one of his own team mates. The colours were interesting, the song was interesting, and there was something about the team that was quite exciting.'

When Ross received a call in 1998 from the WA Football Commission to ask whether he'd be interested in a board position with the Dockers, he agreed to a meeting in Fremantle, where he was told that in fact it was the chairman's position that was on offer. Ross discussed it with his family and his employer (he was deputy CEO of the Chamber of Commerce and Industry of WA) and agreed to take the job. Ross participated in helping raise capital from donors, and Fremantle's generous membership, to realise the Dockers clubrooms at Fremantle Oval, making sure that the new building reflected and drew upon the port city's rich football heritage. It was important to him that new players to the club realised that they were part of a longer football tradition, beyond the few years of the AFL team's existence. This was no easy thing, given the traditional rivalries between the port's two WAFL teams, but in the end the facilities referenced and represented the two footballing families, despite the oval remaining the home ground of the South Fremantle Bulldogs.

Unfortunately for Ross, this period also marked the nadir of the team's on-field fortunes. In 2001, the team lost all of their preseason games and didn't chalk up a win until round eighteen of the home-and-away season. There followed an inadvertent salary-cap breach that further tarnished the club, and damaged its capacity to reap the fullest benefits of the draft system. All of these things led to a fair degree of fan discontent.

It's an anomaly of the West Australian system that the boards for both AFL clubs are appointed by the WAFC. According to Ross, this system is a good commercial model, but it's not a great club model. Members' discontent and a sense of alienation from the decision-making process led to the creation of the Freo Mob, and ultimately the tabling of the *Crawford Report*, and the inaugurating of the reforms enabling members to elect two board members, something that Ross was pleased with. Despite this, those years as chairman were 'the three toughest years of my life I reckon. It was a very hard time.' With both WA-based AFL teams travelling well in recent years, both financially and on the field, it's easy to forget how precarious things were for the Dockers back in the early noughties. 'Football clubs and the football industry are very volatile and unstable, because AFL clubs have fixed costs and overheads but their income is derived from memberships and attendance – both things that are directly related to performance. The few victories we had were wonderful, but on our best days we only had fifteen or sixteen thousand people at games. Our membership base at most was about seventeen thousand. God knows they made some noise, and they loved it and it was good, but when you have fanatical fans and a ferocious press it's a toxic mix when things go bad. As far as club management fared, there was always a need for drastic and impetuous change, and so living through that was pretty tough.'

Which put more pressure on the derby games as a means of demonstrating club pride. When Eagles ruckman Michael Gardiner began roughing up then-rookie Matthew Pavlich before the ball was bounced, in what has become known as the Demolition Derby on July 30, 2000; when the Dockers started pulling back a forty-two point Eagles lead in the third quarter; and after Dockers stalwart Dale Kickett, playing in a brace because of a fractured spine, was repeatedly punched and elbowed by Eagles small-man Phil Read – it was on for young and old. The rivalry's worst brawl to date also resulted in one of the most thrilling derby results, when the Dockers prevailed and won by a single point, after the mercurial Clive Waterhouse kicked seven goals. The Dockers fans and coaching staff were thrilled, as was Ross McLean. 'I remember after the game I was feeling so happy, but was immediately deflated when Tony Peek of the AFL Commission came up to me and said he was disgusted by the game – by the poor sportsmanship, and that he'd be reporting us to the AFL. I just said, "Well, I'm sorry, I thought it was a wonderful game. Footy's tough." And then he went and spoke to Damian Drum, who said it was one of the best victories he'd ever seen in AFL football. We were put under notice by the AFL, but we didn't worry about that too much.'

The aftermath of the game was poignant too because of the tribunal penalty given to Dale Kickett, who was suspended for nine games. That was a great pity, according to Ross, because it's unfair that the career of such a great player, 'the bravest player we've ever had, and a quiet and polite and lovely young man,' should to some fans be defined by what happened in that game. 'He got flattened so often – he just backed into packs and he's such a lovely guy, an all-time favourite of the club, so he shouldn't be ashamed of what happened that day – instead I hope he's proud of his career.'

The memory of the stirring win and Dale Kickett's true character draws a wry smile, and a final memory from Ross. It's an image that marks a clear distinction, as he saw it then, between the two clubs. 'It was something important that I noticed when the Footy Commission took me to the final Dockers game in 1998, just before I became chairman. At that time during the Eagles games, the half-time entertainment was Karl Langdon in a gold lamé jacket surrounded by dancing girls in a Las Vegas sort of crass display.' But on that day in 1998, for the Dockers game half-time entertainment they had 'Noongar poet Jack Davis reading his poetry. If you're talking cultural differences between the clubs, you can't get more telling than that.'

Then Ross laughs, and leans back in his seat. 'Mind you, we were playing Port Adelaide that game. And we got thrashed.'

KEVIN CROON – DOCKERS

Kevin Croon is a Dockers fan but that is because he was forced to choose. He was an inaugural Eagles member, and an inaugural Dockers member, and for many years he went to both teams' home games, until it became untenable. Because he lives in Fremantle, and because his business is headquartered there on Essex Street, he came down on the side of his local team and the rest is history. It's long been a feature of the festivities in Fremantle that when the Dockers make a final, Kevin decks out his business, The Roof & Wall Doctor, in a much-celebrated display of purple pride. There are television cameras and banners and garlands and inside, his staff deck themselves out in purple, despite only some of them supporting the Dockers.

'They do it,' he laughs, because 'they like their jobs.'

The walls in Kevin's office are covered in signed Dockers jumpers and All Blacks memorabilia, reflecting his New Zealander birth. Born in 1945 in Lower Hutt, part of the first wave of what became the baby boomer generation, he grew up 'travelling around, living in transit camps, and then my mum and dad bought what you would call a state house, in an area whose Perth equivalent is probably Balga.' Kevin left school when he was fifteen, at a time when his life was all about rock'n'roll, and rugby. 'I was an Elvis fan and then I loved The Beatles. At school, learning what the main export industry of India was, or whatever, I just didn't want to know. I started a band when I was fifteen and for six years I played five or six nights a week, and worked full-time as well in my dad's business as an earthmoving contractor. There were nights without sleep, but my dad was a hard taskmaster, and so I was always there at seven am to work on time.'

Kevin ended up running his own civil engineering and earthworks company, and by his thirties employed eighty men. A large project that fell through led him and his wife Lavanah to look to move overseas. By a process of elimination that had a lot to do with climate and opportunity, the couple ended up in Perth with their seven-year-old daughter.

Their first home was in Nedlands. Kevin went and watched a couple of local rugby games, but 'when I went to a match on a Saturday they all sat in their cars like they do in New Zealand, and tooted their horns, and there was no one there, so I thought I'm not watching this.'

By chance, Kevin was invited by a friend to watch his first game of Aussie Rules at East Perth Oval. It was Barry Cable's four-hundredth game, and the atmosphere was terrific. What Kevin remembers, however, is 'that at half-time I got up to leave, but nobody else did. I didn't know there were four quarters!'

By virtue of his status as an apprentice fan, having not grown up with the fierce tribal loyalties of the local league, Kevin took up following two WAFL teams rather than one: Claremont, because he lived in the area, and South Fremantle, because his business was there, and they had 'fantastic players like Stephen Michael and Benny Vigona.' He went to all the games, although found out the hard way that wearing a Claremont shirt while walking past the McDonald Stand at Bassendean Oval was a sure way to get yourself spattered with garbage and abuse. Despite that, he found the community he was after in the Claremont members area, 'where there was really good camaraderie and fellowship and where a thousand fans or so would pack the bar. Then the players came and mingled after the game, and it was a really good introduction to the Aussie Rules family.'

He also became a fast fan of the local game. 'Unlike rugby, I loved the fact that I could see the ball at every moment. It's a very good game to watch, especially when Claremont had players like Graham Moss and the Krakouer brothers.' Kevin thinks to this day Graham Moss would be the best football player he's ever seen, and that Dwayne Lamb the toughest player.

It was the seemingly constant loss of the WAFL's best players to the VFL, such as the Krakouer brothers and Wayne Blackwell (although Stephen Michael was a notable exception) that made Kevin interested in the West Coast Eagles when they joined the AFL – the opportunity to watch the best local talent every week. He bought three fifteen-hundred-dollar debenture shares in the company that was 'Eagles Inc.' and went to their first game, and every game after that, including the 1991 grand final, which they lost. When the Dockers came along, he became a Harbour Master member and began supporting them too, until the logistics of supporting both teams came to dominate his weekend. But there are other reasons, too, and have to do with the Dockers' early underdog status and his respect for their struggles. 'The Eagles were helped so much by priority picks, whereas the Dockers started out with nothing until Gerard Neesham took half the Claremont team with him. The AFL seems to have made everything hard for the Dockers, and they've always had poor press from the AFL, because in my opinion the Dockers were formed mainly because Victorians were so worried about the Eagles being unbeatable.'

And then there's the matter of the team cultures, which are according to Kevin 'completely different. I'm a dyed-in-the-wool, have a pie, have a beer, go the footy team, kind of guy. Where I used to sit at Eagles home games, the people around me were more conservative. But when I went to Dockers games I found the people were more like me – passionate dyed-in-the-wool fans despite coming from all walks of life. The bloke on my right – I've been sitting next to him for twenty years. There's a huge camaraderie there with the people who sit around me – things I never saw with the Eagles. There's much, much more atmosphere. When Freo won their first home final here, on our return we packed out all the trains, and there was singing and goodwill. All the bars and cafes of Fremantle were full and the streets full of tooting cars. It was fantastic, because as a team and as fans we now had a city to be in. When the Eagles won the flag in 1992 they had a gathering in Forrest Square in Perth, and it was full of people, but Fremantle has a heart and soul, and the people who live here are proud of this place.'

It was a chance meeting at a Dockers function that introduced Kevin to his favourite Dockers player: Dale Kickett. By way of conversation, Kevin asked Dale what kind of music he liked, and Dale responded, 'Oh, you wouldn't like my music. I like AC/DC.'

This made Kevin laugh, because Kevin has been to every AC/DC concert possible – twelve over the years. He has a tattoo of Bon Scott on his upper arm, and visits Bon's grave at Fremantle Cemetery to mark every year since his passing and his birthday. He asked Dale if he played guitar, but Dale replied, 'Nope, nobody's ever showed me.' If Dale bought himself a guitar, Kevin said, then he'd teach him, and for the next while Dale turned up every Monday afternoon at Kevin's work to learn guitar chords, as did four other Indigenous Dockers players. When Dale was involved in the Demolition Derby brawl in 2000, Kevin chided him, and not because of the aggression, but because 'my biggest concern is there's you, a budding Jimi Hendrix, using these guitar fingers to punch someone in the head. I said, "Mate, that's not what we do. You break your fingers, you'll be playing two-fingered guitar, and that's no good."'

For the first few years of the derbies, Kevin refused to go and watch the games, basically because of mixed feelings, until he made the mistake of lending his tickets to a man he didn't realise was an Eagles fan. His friend in the neighbouring seat soon rang him up and complained that the guy was 'feral'. Kevin afterwards confronted the troublemaker and said, 'I thought you were a Dockers supporter?' to which the man replied, 'I am when they're playing someone else, but when they're playing the Eagles, I'm Eagles.' Needless to say, the wolf in sheep's clothing was never invited to use the season tickets again, and Kevin began going to the derby games too.

He has a regular bet of fifty dollars on the derby games with a workmate called Terry who follows the Eagles. Over the years, when the Dockers were on a winning streak, Kevin ended up collecting twelve fifty-dollar notes which he kept in his desk drawer, each note marked 'Given by Terry – Dockers beat Eagles.' Terry got his revenge a few years later, however, when Kevin called a 'team photo' of all the staff at the Freo office of The Roof & Wall Doctor. 'All my guys stood out the front of the office for the photograph, and we were just in normal gear and the photographer came and went and when I eventually looked at the photo, I saw an Eagles scarf hanging on the fence. I said to Terry, "Mate, you've stuffed up my photo – about three grand's worth," but I wasn't having an Eagles scarf in there, so I had to get the photographer back, and it cost me another three grand, but it was worth it just to get the Eagles stuff out of it.'

Kevin's not beyond engaging in a bit of missionary behaviour either. A few years ago All Blacks legend Buck Shelford was in town, and Kevin offered to take him to a Dockers game. 'He's the most famous and most loved of the All Blacks captains – the one who resurrected the haka. I took him to a Dockers game against Melbourne and there I was, “Kevin the Kiwi”, sitting with Buck Shelford on one side and WA footy legend John Todd on the other. Buck loved the game – the Dockers played good open footy on that day and they won. Buck kept saying to me, “Mate, if I had of seen this game as a young boy, this would suit me. You can see the ball and it doesn’t matter if you’re big or small, there’s a position for everybody. And how fit are they?”’

There is a derby-day ritual that Kevin follows to the letter. He knows that it takes precisely an hour to get from his home in South Fremantle to his seat at Subiaco Oval. ‘So I get dressed up in all my gear and I drive into Fremantle, and I park my car behind my workplace here. Then I like to walk through Freo town. The place is always buzzing, and so I like to walk through the town and say g’day to everyone, and “Go Dockers”, and that kind of thing. Then I get on the train using my member’s ticket as payment. The trains leave every fifteen minutes and on the train there are people singing and dancing and that’s very enjoyable. I like to get to the ground early. I get off at the same station, and enter the same gate, and walk up the same stairs to my seat. I just watch the ground fill up and I don’t go for beers or anything – I just sit there.’

Winning is important to all Dockers fans but is always extra poignant for Kevin. He’s never in a hurry to leave the ground, because then he might miss the voice of his rock idol, Bon Scott. While he doesn’t see the Eagles club or fans giving Bon Scott the same respect, because they ‘are probably more One Direction fans,’ when the speakers boom out ‘TNT’ after a Dockers win, Kevin waves goodbye and says his silent prayer: ‘Bon, if you’re up there son and looking down, I know you feel honoured by these forty-two thousand singing your song and hearing your voice.’

There’s no doubt in Kevin’s mind. Bon Scott is definitely a Dockers fan.

GREIG JOHNSTON – EAGLES

Greig Johnston has that most enviable of jobs – he's a sportswriter for a national website called *The New Daily*. Mirroring the transition seen in the United States, where the gradual dying off of the traditional long-form sports report correlated with a resurgence of the best sports journalism appearing on media websites like ESPN, Greig has been part of the same evolution here in Australia. He's the sports editor, administering the site, and I've read some of his work over the years including a terrific profile on the occasion of Chris Judd's retirement called 'The greatest game you didn't see Chris Judd play'. The piece describes newly drafted Eagles recruit Chris Judd's legendary sole game for East Perth, before he graduated to the Eagles' starting twenty-two. Predictably, Judd blitzed the game, and his pace and verve and courageous tackling provoked awe in everyone who witnessed the spectacle. He had possessions up in the high thirties, kicked four goals and was clearly best on ground. His coach, Tony Micale (who souvenired Judd's guernsey), when presenting the award in front of the gathered members, said to the crowd, 'Have a good look at him, guys, because we'll never see him again.' Fortunately for the Fremantle Dockers, Eagles coach John Worsfold had opted to leave their number-one draft pick out of the derby team he chose for that day. (It didn't matter – the Eagles won by nineteen points, but clearly it could have been by a lot more.)

Greig has just returned from a few years working in

Melbourne. He's in his thirties and has a baby daughter and wanted to be close to his and his wife's family. It's a big move in terms of his career, but it's also a beautiful spring afternoon in Leederville, and Greig doesn't mind at all. He's also used to big moves, his family having emigrated to Perth from Glasgow when he was ten years old. Sports in the old country was about Glasgow Rangers FC and boxing in the era of Barry McGuigan and Frank Bruno – his dad took him to his first heavyweight bout when Greig was seven. In his new home of Morley, Greig played soccer for the Morley Windmills and Dianella Serbia, but in the background, the Perth Wildcats were taking off and so were the West Coast Eagles. Greig's Scottish uncle was a Swan Districts fan and took Greig to see his first game of football out at Bassendean. He remembers not understanding the rules but being amazed at the talents of Troy Ugle, 'an Indigenous guy who could jump over tall buildings with a single bound.'

Australian Rules was something that Greig absorbed osmotically, by way of sports radio. 'My dad used to listen to racing radio with Darren McCauley, and they would commentate on the football too, and so I sort of got used to the rhythms of the game through listening to it on the radio.' Meanwhile, a mate from school was teaching Greig the hands-on and performative aspects of the game. 'I had a friend called Tim Dunn at Illawarra Primary School in Ballajura, and he introduced me to the concept of kick-to-kick in his backyard. I had no idea how to hold the ball and I used to kick it lengthways – I just had no idea. But Tim'd kick it and he'd slide in and take a mark and he'd shout, "Dunstall!" Or he'd take a hang and shout, "Capper!" Or "Watson!", or "Madden!" And I used to think, what's this guy on about?'

Despite being a new arrival in the country, it didn't take Greig too long to buy into the anti-Victorian feeling that had long been a part of WA's sporting culture and, for so many, a good reason to support the West Coast Eagles. 'If you watched Channel Seven on a Sunday morning they had a show called *Sportsworld* or something, with Don Scott and Sandy Roberts, and Don Scott in particular occupied the role that Robert Walls has taken on lately – he had no time for anything that wasn't Victorian. We bought into the general resentment, and I remember there were anti–Don Scott banners at the games, and it was all about anti-Victorian sentiment and it was very tribal – us against them.'

At a time when it was still possible for the average punter to buy tickets at the gate for an Eagles game, Greig began to attend the home fixtures and learn the code. He still wasn't full bottle on the rules, but that didn't diminish his appreciation for the game or his favourite players. His favourites weren't the usual suspects of Kemp, Matera and Jakovich, but had everything to do with his own sense of someone lacking the silky skills of the naturally talented. 'I liked Stevan Jackson who played centre half-forward, and Tony Evans. My favourite current player is Patrick McGinnity, who you know is roundly pilloried. It was Peter Wilson, not Ben Cousins. Peter Sumich, if you want to talk about flawed genius. He used to cop so much shit for his kicking, but that night he kicked thirteen against Footscray – it was a great night. To me it's like if I wandered into an AFL club and tried to get a kick – the Rocky story but in footy format.'

When the Fremantle Dockers arrived on the scene, there was no chance of Greig switching teams, although one of his best friends did. 'The weird thing is, I could understand you jumping ship if you grew up supporting East or South Fremantle, but he grew up supporting West Perth, so I'm not sure what happened there. I think he was just looking for something new. But I felt like I'd been there in the early years, and we'd won a couple of flags and even if Fremantle had been given draft concessions like the GWS and Gold Coast did later, I still wouldn't have done it. Switching teams was never a consideration on my part, but I didn't wish Fremantle ill until much later.'

As far as derby rivalry goes, like many Eagles fans, Greig was initially bemused by the determination of the new team on the block to thump their older cousins. 'I remember there was a weird thing on the radio one day, when Gerard Neesham was asked who the Dockers wanted to play in their first game. Neesham answered, "We'd like to play Eagles round one at Subiaco" and I remember thinking, "Mate, you'll get thumped. We're the premiers."'

Again, like many Eagles fans, it wasn't until Fremantle tasted derby success and began to win regularly that any strong feeling developed. 'I used to watch Freo beat Sydney quite often, and guys like Craig Callaghan were playing great footy, and I'd certainly barrack for Freo, whereas now I'd certainly barrack against Freo. The derby rivalry has developed pretty organically, and I guess Fremantle just got tired of being pushed around. I still remember that first derby win in 1999, with Tony Modra snapping the goal and slapping the ground, and knowing at that stage that the game was gone – they just weren't going to be denied. It was the first derby win and a huge, huge monkey off the back. And then there's the Demolition Derby. Y'know, Michael Gardiner's not one of my favourite people, but I do feel a bit defensive about what happened on that day, with him pushing rookie Matthew Pavlich around. Because I remember Gardiner's first game against Footscray, when four Bulldogs players just went for him all game, and he was just trying to do the same. I also particularly remember that game when the Carr brothers basically made Ben Cousins suffer for the day, and Josh Carr won the Glendinning Medal for doing that.'

Favourite Eagles players who've stood up in derby games include Michael Braun, 'one of those blokes who nobody remembers, but that's what happens when you're fourth wheel after Judd, Cousins and Kerr. I remember in one derby Peter Bell and another guy trying to go after Judd, and he just slipped through them and they've hit each other because Judd was untouchable. He's the best I've ever seen in terms of his pace, and he always played well in big games.' Greig found the sacking from the club of Matt Rosa in 2015 pretty disappointing. This observation leads him back to the subject of being a sportswriter. While still a student in Curtin University's journalism course, he was sent to work with the East Perth Football Club and developed a fondness for the club, and a greater appreciation for the game. Because he's now a professional writer, however, covering all of the teams in the AFL league, as well as numerous other sports, it's important that he not be seen to play favourites. 'I'm harsher on the things I love, and I'm harsher about the Eagles for that reason. I don't want to be seen as sycophantic to their cause.'

Greig moved away from Perth for pragmatic reasons, essentially because there are more media outlets over East. As his thoughts turn to the coming seasons, and how he's going to approach supporting his team, he reflects on one unintended benefit from when he worked in Melbourne. 'If you're not an Eagles member and you live *here,* you can't see them play. But in Melbourne, I only missed a couple of games around the time when my daughter Lola was born.' Asked to describe the atmosphere of the Eagles away games, however, Greig responds: 'In a word, *dead.* There's no atmosphere. Eagles versus Melbourne at the MCG? It's the definition of flat. It's dreadful, absolutely dreadful. You can hear a pin drop.'

But like a true fan, there are always positives to be found. 'This will tell you a bit about my psychology, but one of the most enjoyable years of footy I've ever had was back in 2010 when we won the wooden spoon. I reckon the reason for that is, if you're shithouse you see the positives in everything. Like it's, oh geez, that was a great smother by young Scott Selwood – he could really be something one day. You go there expecting nothing so you can't be disappointed.'

A fan who likes the quirky player over the superstar, and an underdog team who struggles, over a team expected to achieve great things? I suggest to Greig that he sounds like a long-suffering Dockers supporter, but his answer is drowned out by the sound of traffic.

MARIA CAMPOREALE – DOCKERS

Maria Camporeale has lived most of her life in Fremantle, and that's because whenever she's away from the port city, she misses it so much that she soon returns. Stints out in the country working as a schoolteacher, and elsewhere in Perth, have never lasted for long. Born in Italy, Maria moved to Australia when she was four years old. A year in Geraldton was followed by two years in Wittenoom, where her father caught asbestosis, although fortunately he never developed mesothelioma.

The family settled in South Fremantle 'and that's been part of my identity ever since. Being from Fremantle is really, really important to me. So even when I'm away it doesn't matter – I'm still from Fremantle.' Maria grew up within walking distance of Fremantle Oval, and naturally followed the Bulldogs in the WAFL league. 'We were very tribal in those days. People you normally spoke to in quite a civil manner before the football season started suddenly became your worst enemy. When we moved into a house with a telephone, I remember my father and his friends, depending on who won the Freo derby, would give each other a ring. So you had bragging rights going way back then. On derby weeks you would walk down the street in Fremantle, and the shops would have bunting – mostly South Fremantle colours but some shops had East Fremantle flags. We lived in South Fremantle, and East Fremantle was like a foreign country. There were only a few people we knew who lived there, and you'd always follow the team of the place where you were born, and you didn't have a lot of intermarriage as you do now. The best Saturdays of my adolescent life were spent at Fremantle Oval, although we were allowed to go away as far as East Fremantle on the bus for the derby.'

Maria's father worked down in Kwinana, but on the weekends he could also be found at Fremantle Oval, watching the game with his friends, standing in front of the old grandstand, meaning that Maria had to behave 'because everybody knew somebody who knew you or your parents.' Maria sat beside the covered shelter down at the Fremantle Market end. Her friends were the same girls who set up the first South Fremantle cheer squad, and together they 'never missed a game, even when it was raining. We used to sit on the stone steps and boo people like Austin Robertson who never missed a goal, and Bill Walker and others. I used to love watching Danny Sidic, Brian Ciccotosto and Stephen Michael, and all of our Indigenous players, because we had many great Indigenous players on our team then.'

Maria started her teaching career in 1978, and was posted out to Wyalkatchem, but she always made sure to return to Fremantle for the weekends. 'What I love about Fremantle is its position on the coast, the light, and the ocean, and the football oval right there in the middle of town. Everywhere else I lived, I felt out of my element. In Fremantle, you knew everybody on the streets.'

When Maria was posted to Karratha, the option of driving home for the weekend to see family and watch the football was gone. As a result, when the AFL competition started and the Eagles arrived on the scene, it wasn't on her radar. 'I didn't have a passion for it, and I heard that it decimated the WAFL. I grew up going to WAFL games where every game was packed out. Where the umpires came out onto the ground they had to put a chicken-wire fence over them because people used to pelt the umpires with tomatoes.

It seemed like the Eagles had nothing to do with me, or Fremantle, and I felt disconnected from them. And they had such terrible colours. I used to call them the Chicken Treat team because the original Chicken Treat colours were yellow and blue.'

But when Fremantle entered the competition it was a different story. Maria moved back to Fremantle, although she didn't have the money to renew her vehicle insurance, let alone take out a Dockers membership. She went to the occasional game, and otherwise watched every match on the television. Meanwhile, her initial suspicions about the West Coast Eagles were being confirmed in her workplace. Fremantle's early years were notoriously difficult, and despite maintaining her loyalty and commitment within the crucible of consistent losses and the odd stirring victory, it was very easy for Eagles fans to ridicule the struggling team and their stubborn fans.

Even when Fremantle began winning derbies, this only made things worse in the context of several seasons that went nowhere. 'The charge could always be made that Fremantle's focus on the derbies as their grand finals was vaguely ridiculous, and the closest they'd ever get to a grand final anyway.' When students in Maria's high-school English classes ridiculed her love for the 'Dorkers', she had no choice but to forgive them, as misguided souls. She wore her purple scarf every Friday, to the point that the kids in class knew which day of the week it was because Maria was wearing purple. Even after a humiliating weekend loss, she often wore the scarf on Monday too, 'because it was important to stand up for the team.' It was when a colleague's constant childish teasing became personal that Maria drew her own line in the sand, and threatened to put in an official grievance. 'I couldn't remain ambivalent about West Coast anymore because of their aggro supporters. A lot of people like me became solidified in our faith because of that sneering attitude towards the Dockers. Now when somebody's goading starts to affect me, I just go, "Stop right there!"'

Maria discovered 'bill-smoothing' and thereby the ability to pay for season tickets. She talked her son, and her partner (who until then had shown no interest in sport) into joining her, and they've been going together ever since. Derbies are always special occasions because of the anxiety involved with 'knowing you're going to get paid out on severely on Monday if we lose.' She spends derby week in a state of 'suspended animation', because one thing that's never gone away is that the derby is 'just like a sacrament, speaking as a secular Catholic.' Maria doesn't ever bet with colleagues on the outcome of the game, because that would be asking for trouble. 'I'm not superstitious about anything else but I'm incredibly superstitious when it comes to football.' On game day Maria wears purple. 'Purple earrings, a purple amethyst ring and a necklace that reads FAITH, HOPE AND CHARITY. I have silver charms that have a Dockers heart with an anchor on it, and a purple amethyst in the middle that's got to be worn, even though I don't wear religious amulets although of course, being Italian, I have them. And I don't wear my football scarf – I wear a dressy purple one.' She doesn't want any 'extra energy' diverted from her focus on the game, and so doesn't prepare any food for a derby game beyond a thermos of Italian coffee and some biscotti, 'but if it's a really important derby I don't even do that, because I feel like I'm going to be sick. I just try and keep everything really low-key, so that there's no drama to distract me.'

Maria goes to the Dockers Doig Medal award presentation every year, where she gets to meet the players, who she's always impressed by as 'lovely and polite young men.' Asked to list her favourites she begins with Lachie Neale, Michael

Johnson and Nat Fyfe, then gives up when she realises she's going to list the whole team, because 'to be honest I love them all you know. They all play with such heart.'

Asked tongue-in-cheek whether she's done any missionary work in the school system, converting impressionable young minds to the Dockers cause, Maria laughs. She has convinced a non–sports loving colleague to at least watch the Dockers games, who's enjoyed them so much that 'he's in the bag', but more importantly, 'I've validated some of my students who were closet Fremantle supporters but who were too embarrassed to admit it back in the tough days. I gave them confidence to declare themselves, and now that Fremantle are doing well some of the kids openly go, "Miss, I go to the football too, where do you sit?"'

On the occasion of her recent birthday, Maria's family was stuck with the problem of buying a present for someone 'who's got everything I need. I said I don't need a birthday present, we'll just have lunch or something.' In a stroke of genius, her son found her some Dockers licence plates, numbered 1307. The number might be unimportant to another, but for Maria it was 'perfect and beautiful', and meant to be. 'Thirteen was Tendai Mzungu, and seven is Nat Fyfe, and we were there when he played his first game. We feel like we've grown up with him and, you know, he's grown up with us.'

RON ELLIOTT – EAGLES

Ron Elliott, lately a filmmaker and novelist, is still a Bassendean boy at heart. His first memory of football is going to Swan Districts games with his father, sitting on a wooden bench near the fence eating hot chips while protecting his head from the rain with a newspaper. The football was a terrific experience – he got to see the great Billy Walker in his prime, but what really sticks in Ron's memory is the journey there. 'For me it was more about getting on the train and catching the train with my dad, then getting off the train and walking to the ground with the other supporters. It's like the tributaries gather as you get closer to the ground, and the groups of people get closer together, and suddenly you're part of this stream going into the ground.'

Later, when Ron was a uni student studying to become a teacher and living at UWA's residential college Currie Hall (after he convinced the Education Department that Middle Swan was too far to commute, receiving lodging and board on his way to becoming a 'bonded teacher'), he became a regular attendee at WAFL games played at Leederville and Subiaco ovals. What was great about the WAFL was the size of the crowds (tiny Leederville Oval knew crowds of thirty thousand fans), the sense of being packed alongside everyone else but also because 'in those days, most grounds you went to had a high proportion of opposition supporters and there was a lot of banter, the throwing of witty abuse, and that's something that's gone missing out of Perth for quite a while now. It's like, all the aggro was out on the field and the banter was always quite generous and amusing, with people calling out clever remarks and everybody around you going, "Ah, good one mate," and admiring the wit. There was more of a sense of community, and it was a lot more fun.'

By that point in his life, plenty of the boys Ron had grown up with, or knew at university, were playing league for different WAFL teams. Ron's best mate's big brother, Stephen Skulley, was playing for the Swans on the wing, and one of his peers at Currie Hall was playing centre half-forward for the Swans, while another mate from high school, Donny Holmes, ended up playing for the Eagles.

Ron's two great sporting loves were the staples – footy and cricket (Ron's first novel, *Spinner*, is the story of a cricketing child prodigy born in country WA), but his particular skills lent themselves to basketball, a game he played until only recently. He continued with his university studies by beginning an honours degree in English literature, but due to an interest in film, began studying film at Curtin University at the same time. Two years into his degrees across two institutions he decided he had to choose, and became a writer and filmmaker, winning awards along the way and producing the feature film *Justice*, set entirely in Fremantle. He lived for a time in Tasmania, working for the ABC, and then in Sydney, all the while looking for a football club to hang his hat on. He went to Sydney games, and supported North Melbourne, but returned to Perth in time to raise a young family and witness the birth of the West Coast Eagles. Ron attended many of the home fixtures and watched all of their two-hundred-odd games before the Fremantle Dockers 'were invented'. The usual perception of the Eagles having it easy in those years is a blatant misconception, as far as Ron is concerned. 'I've been there from the beginning and before the beginning. We lost game after game in the beginning. I remember one game where we were flogged by

St Kilda, and we only scored three points in the first half – it was famous. So now it shits me when people say, "Oh, you're just high-flyers, you've jumped on some bandwagon." We didn't play Fremantle for seven years. We won two grand finals, and we had a journey, and there were other villains in our narrative, and other things that had gone on. We had to fight battles about travel, and we had to fight battles about where finals were played. Those were things that Fremantle just inherited, but that we had to fight for.'

Ron's broad thesis vis-à-vis the rivalry between the two West Australian teams is that 'we're an integral part of Fremantle's identity, but Fremantle is not an integral part of ours.' As a filmmaker and novelist, Ron identifies the journey each club has taken with broad narrative arcs that intersect on derby days. For Ron, the plot points, or major turning points, in the derby narrative, consist of four important derbies. The first was Fremantle's initial win in 1999, when Tony Modra kicked a goal from the pocket while being tackled, and celebrated by beating the ground. The second derby turning point, following Fremantle's first derby drubbing by 117 points in 2000, was the notorious Demolition Derby. The Eagles loss by one point was a pity, but he could understand the Fremantle tactics. 'If one team's got too far ahead, really, it's not right, but the only thing to try to do was level it by being physical. So you've actually got to throw that in.' The third important derby moment was Hayden Ballantyne missing a shot on goal after the siren in 2011, meaning that the Eagles won by a point. Ron speaks of his affection and admiration for some of the Fremantle players, but not for Dockers fans. 'In the beginning I only had fine feelings towards Fremantle. I've always had my favourites in the Fremantle footy team, such as Luke McPharlin and Dale Kickett. I've got the ones I love and the ones I hate, and there's a lot to admire in the current team, as well as past teams.' The derbies really only became interesting, as far as Ron was concerned, when 'the Dockers fans started getting more and more anxious and angry about it, and I started to go, "Oh, this is a bit of fun." It's the fans that give me the shits, and make me want Freo to lose, and I delight every time Fremantle loses now.' He finds the cliché bandied about that brands Eagles fans as chardonnay-sipping elites as hilarious, given his own family background and the varied lives of his Eagles-supporting friends. The occasional bad behaviour and feral attitude of fans from both clubs can be sheeted home not to the clubs themselves or the rivalry that's developed, but more to the fact that 'Perth has changed. There's a level of rudeness and anger now, on the roads and everywhere else. It's not just a case of people being bashed, but that everywhere you go there's people who're aggro.'

The final turning point in the narrative that is the derby games, according to Ron, occurred in the final derby of 2015, when the Dockers and the Eagles were one and two on the ladder and when, because of a depleted backline, and the loss of forward LeCras and ruckman Natanui, the Eagles were expected to lose, but instead ran away twenty-four-point winners. This game was important because in the race to secure a grand final berth, 'Fremantle were the team to measure ourselves against. We needed to know if we were the real deal. And we were, at that point.' It marked the sign of a team on the rise, achieving beyond expectation, but also the evidence of another team on the wane, namely the Dockers, who Ron doesn't think can win the flag under the defensively minded Ross Lyon. Saying that, Ron would welcome a derby grand final, just for the opportunity to beat the Dockers and claim the ultimate bragging rights. But if the Eagles lost, it wouldn't be the end of the world, he acknowledges, at least to the large body of parochial Eagles fans who don't hate the Dockers, and support both teams because, aside from everything else, the Dockers are at least West Australian. 'There are huge numbers of people who aren't as nasty as me, or hate the Dockers as avidly as me, and they would take a grand final loss to the Dockers and move on.'

For Ron, whose regular bet is a bottle of spirits on important games, the loss would sting, but he too could live with it. It would be one more turning point in the ongoing story of the derby, with its heroes and villains, its triumphs and disappointments. And besides, 'so many bottles of spirits have been won and lost over the years.'

JUSTIN LANGER – EAGLES

Talking to Justin Langer, it would be easy to assume that he's a natural Dockers fan. His family has a lot of Fremantle history, he was a South Fremantle supporter in the WAFL as a kid (he has been number-one ticket holder at Subiaco for the last twelve years), he's a good mate of Dockers fans like Geoff Marsh and Wayne Andrews, and he spends a lot of time chatting with Ross Lyon, whom he greatly admires. When he was a child, Justin headed down to Fremantle with his nan and pop, who were born-and-bred Fremantle people – his Nan having grown up in a cottage next door to the Roundhouse – to watch the Bulldogs play and to pay homage to the great red dingo on the flour mill on the way out of town. 'If we won, my nanna, she'd go, "Good win today, Dingo," and if we lost she'd say, "Better luck next week, Dingo." My first childhood memories of the footy are coming down to Fremantle with my nanna, who had a thermos of milk and tea and sandwiches and that was my thing – I got to watch my absolute hero Stephen Michael, and Maurice Rioli and Noel Carter and Paul Mountain, and all those other great players. My grandfather's still alive. He's ninety-four. Just the other day he was telling me about how he lived on High Street, Fremantle, when he was a little kid, and so Fremantle's in his bones.'

Fremantle and the dingo still play a role in Justin's life. 'I come down to Freo every Sunday morning with my second daughter Ali Rose, who's a bit of a hippy. We say, "Peace-out, Captain Fremantle," when we drive past his statue, and the same when we go past the dingo. A bloke who helps me with my money – he helps me with the stock market – I bought him a Dingo Flour Mill cap at the markets recently for good luck, and told him, "Yeah, the dingo's smiling this week, mate."'

Justin lets that sink in before adding, 'That said, I'm an Eagles supporter. And I'm an Eagles supporter because of Guy McKenna, who used to live close by to me in Carine. I used to see this kid with a pair of running shorts and singlet, bouncing this footy around Carine's open spaces, and as a teenager I've just gone: I want to do that one day. And when he started playing for the Eagles, obviously that's when I started barracking for the Eagles. I loved the way he kicked out from goals. Y'know, it's such a little thing, but that's why I love Shannon Hurn now, for the same reason.'

Justin grew up playing both cricket and footy, initially for the Warwick Junior Football Club, and later Alcock Cup footy for Aquinas up until year twelve. One of Australia's most celebrated motivational speakers, Justin still talks 'about the lessons I learned from some of the old coaches in junior footy there. Y'know, I still love the "Eye of the Tiger" and the smell of Dencorub and the atmosphere in footy change rooms.'

Despite being a promising footballer, fate intervened, and in a good way. On a schoolboy tour of England at age sixteen, Justin scored a century on debut at Lords. 'I just remember running around to the old red phone box at Lords, and ringing my mum and dad, and I told them I got a century at Lords, and they were so pumped. And that was the thing while I was over there – I played cricket every day and I kept thinking, "Imagine doing this for a job. Imagine playing cricket every day." And that was when I made my decision to choose cricket. Plus, you get hurt too much playing footy.'

Justin was in Perth during the birth of the Eagles, but

with his first-class career kicking off in 1990 and his test cricket debut touring the West Indies in 1993 he wasn't around for long. His favourite players at that time were of course 'Bluey McKenna and John Worsfold who were just tough, and I've got fond memories of Suma in the early days. And I loved Laurie Keene. And of course Chris Mainwaring. I love Mainy, and I was actually with him on the day he died. We were due to have a charity kickboxing fight on the Wednesday night, and we trained together on the Sunday. He was a bit of a rogue, but I loved the way he went about it.'

It wasn't always easy keeping in touch with the AFL while on overseas tours and playing county cricket, at least not until the invention of the internet. Justin, who worked out that the winter of 2015 was his first winter home in twenty-five years, used to rely upon watching Eagles games on his computer, and occasionally on television. During one tour of India with the WA team in 2006, it nearly went wrong. The Eagles were in the grand final, and the team were assembled watching the game on a television. It was a close game, and with two minutes to go the television went 'Boof! The power went out and then there's blokes running around everywhere, and then with about eight seconds to go it came back on and we fucking won, we won by one point, and we're all jumping up and going wild!'

Winning that grand final was great, but so is winning derby games against Fremantle. 'It's a bit like the Ashes. It's bragging rights isn't it? There's people I work with who are mad Dockers, and when we win we take the piss out of them, and when we lose they take the piss out of us – so it's just about bragging. Your team's only as good as their last game. I enjoy the build-up to the game. It's like a big test match – there's lots of theatre and drama in the lead-up to it. I love every derby game, and I get seriously grumpy if we lose against the Dockers. If we lose, I'm grumpy for a week.'

While he loves going to the games, Justin's routine lately is to watch the footy at home, 'just sitting at home and watching it on the telly.' He understands the game-day superstitions and rituals of fans and players alike, because back when he was playing test cricket for Australia, opening the bat alongside Matthew Hayden against bowlers like Curtly Ambrose and other ferocious quicks, routine was important. 'I was very routine-oriented, you could call them superstitions, and I understand superstitions because sport is so process-oriented. My nan made the best pavlova and cakes because she stuck to the recipe that worked – she didn't put in an extra couple of eggs or an extra bit of sugar. And with my cricket I stuck to my recipe that worked, and that meant what time I got up in the morning, to what I ate in the morning, and the routine I had when I got to the ground. I padded up and sat there with my half a glass of water, and my armguard there, and my helmet and my two pieces of PK chewing gum. It had to be PK – it couldn't be Extra, or Juicy Fruit, or I wouldn't make any runs. And I had my headphones on, and I listened to the same track for the whole series. For one series it was "Lose Yourself" by Eminem, before that I had "She Will Be Loved" by Maroon Five, I had "Big City Life" by Mattafix and Pink's "You and Your Hand". But it had to be the same song per series. Because I was so nervous I'd have a sip of water and then Haydos would say, "Ready to go, little fella?" and I'd say, "Ready to go, big fella?" and then we were away. So I get rituals, and why some people have to sit in their same seat, and my ritual is to sit down in my seat, and have my coffee, and then have my toasted sandwich, and just be normal, mate. Although I'm back on the Extra gum, because my dentist said I've had too many PKs.'

Justin's a bit cagey about betting on sporting outcomes, having made a significant bet with the Warriors team physio a few years ago that a then-unknown, named Nat Fyfe, wouldn't win the Brownlow. He also famously made the promise that if fellow WA player Simon Katich left the state cricket team, 'I'd play the next test nude. That's how adamant I was, and then he did leave. I didn't play the next test nude, but I'm probably a bit smarter about these things as a result.'

Apart from cricket, and his current role as coach of the Warriors and the Scorchers, and occasional stand-in coach for the Australian cricket team, Justin keeps fit by training in martial arts. Batting and fighting always seemed complementary because, 'when you're both batting and fighting you've got to have good technique, good footwork, good concentration and the courage to face your own demons.' In the ring and on the pitch, 'you've got nowhere to hide.' In martial arts you have to attack in order to defend, 'or be steamrolled', and the same can be said for football. Justin cites the example of his friend Chris Mainwaring, who was a second dan Zen Do Kai martial artist. 'Second dan is a marathon grading – it's thirty two-minute rounds. It's hardcore and Mainy did it – he was like a bull.' Justin's own experience sparring with Danny Green was 'the most intimidating thing I've ever done – he hit me twice in the liver and it was like being hit by a shotgun.' The image of a smaller man facing a larger opponent without fear or hesitation brings Dockers players Hayden Ballantyne and Lachie Neale to mind: 'little guys who just have a red-hot dip, running, crashing into these big blokes without fear.' Justin feels for him, because of that pivotal derby moment in 2011 when Ballantyne missed a difficult shot on goal from the boundary line, resulting in a one-point loss to the Dockers. Justin once hit a six on ninety-five to bring up his ton, in front of ninety thousand people at the MCG, in an Ashes series – the ultimate in cricket glory. But it isn't the glory that Justin describes as memorable or important. 'It's the perfection of knowing, for a split second, something that no one else knows. I stood there with my arms up before it's gone for six, because I knew.' What was a comic moment for many Eagles supporters, with Hayden Ballantyne celebrating an after-the-siren derby win with an impossible kick, draws only sympathy from Justin. 'That'd be like me hitting the ball and going *yeaahh*, and at the last moment the breeze blows it back in and I get caught. Ballantyne must have *known*, and he must've felt ripped off, because that was one moment in his life when he knew something no one else did, and we're all holding our breath like when you're a kid being held underwater, but he got ripped off, and that doesn't happen very often in your life.'

Despite his admiration for Ballantyne, Lachie Neale, Ross Lyon and others on the Dockers team, following the Eagles and having the Dockers as your second team is 'frog shit'. There's also a second reason why Justin's an Eagles fan. 'I just love that we're so parochial in Western Australia. We love Western Australia, but it comes down to north and south of the river, doesn't it? I wouldn't dream of living south of the river, because I've lived north of the river all my life. And that's what I love about the derby. I've got so much time and respect and so much history with Freo, but we're split when it comes to north and south of the river, and the Eagles and the Dockers. I love Freo, but I don't love them, because I'm an Eagles supporter.'

GABY HADDOW – EAGLES

Gaby Haddow has recently become a grandmother for the first time, but she's not the sort of Eagles fan to indulge in draping Eagles colours around the little one's cot, or to croon the club song as lullaby. She figures that her granddaughter will come to the winter game on her own terms, although Gaby plans to take her to Eagles games when she's older, if she's keen.

Gaby came to football by going to Claremont games with her father. This was during the early '80s when Claremont, as well as Swan Districts and South Fremantle, were one of the WAFL powerhouses. She enjoyed the day out, 'unless we were playing Swan Districts at Bassendean Oval, when it got a bit rowdy.' Claremont had a great team, with Graham Moss and Warren Ralph, but Gaby particularly admired the Krakouer brothers, who were soon to depart for the VFL. As a young student, she lived in share houses with footy-mad friends and got to know about the Victorian league that way, although she didn't have much choice in the matter. 'The VFL was a major thing for a lot of the blokes. At one stage they had all those Sunday morning footy shows where they just talked footy endlessly, and in one of the houses I shared, they had two televisions sitting on top of one another playing different footy shows at the same time.'

Gaby is currently an academic specialising in the area of information studies, but back then she was studying to become a librarian. She continued to take her two children to Claremont games, but when the family moved to Canberra during the period that West Coast Eagles entered a newly national competition, the Eagles didn't really make much of an impact in the rugby-loving territory. Gaby had to wait until the early '90s when she returned to Perth, to rekindle her interest in football. The Eagles were the only show in town, and they were enjoying a period of dramatic success, winning two grand finals in four years. 'Most of Perth supported the Eagles back then. I remember during the 1992 grand final, the newspaper had a shot of the freeway, and it was completely deserted. All the shops across Perth were decked out in Eagles colours.'

This success and widespread support was threatened however when the Dockers came along. 'The Eagles had already established their place, but they must have felt threatened because you know plenty of people jumped, once the Dockers came along. My father-in-law had always been a very strong Eagles supporter, but his heart was in Fremantle, so when the Dockers came along, he became a Docker.'

Gaby's affections remained with the Eagles, and it was a chance meeting at a party that brought her into contact with someone from the club. Gaby was completing her honours in library studies, and she asked whether anyone was looking after all of the Eagles memorabilia, 'or at least putting it together. Brian Cook was approached and they asked me to do it, and paid me to do it.'

Being the Eagles official memorabilia coordinator was a casual role, 'but a lot of fun. At that stage the Eagles clubrooms were still on the railway side of the ground, and they had all of the honour boards there, and they had quite a lot of stuff already. What mostly interested me was the kit from the two grand finals. Obviously, they weren't going to lose the premiership cups, but there was a risk of losing other material not recognised as important then. There were other things that I discovered as I went along, and spoke to those people from the club who could make time to see me. I found out they had a collection of newspaper clippings, and I asked the CEO to go through them with me, and decide what was important. If there were years missing, then I'd go to the State Library and search through the rolls of film. I collected all of this material in albums made of quality acid-free paper. Nowadays you'd just scan them digitally, but they did look good.'

Most of the work consisted of indexing the vast amount of material, from videos to newspaper articles, and photographs and jumpers, though not all of the people Gaby interviewed or made enquiries with were happy. 'I got a warmer reception from some than others. Some were busy, and others didn't see the point of what I was doing.'

Regardless, the work continued. Some of the finds were interesting. 'They had a jar of soil from the MCG, taken on the first grand-final day, and there were player newsletters and there was a members magazine as well. I collected up all of the guernseys and stuff like that, and made sure it was all properly wrapped.'

Some of this retrieved material was later put on display at the Eagles clubrooms at Subiaco Oval, including what was probably the strangest piece of memorabilia Gaby collected, now kept in the foyer of the club, perched on a length of jam tree. 'When someone rang up the club and said, "I've got a stuffed eagle", it was suggested that I should collect it. It was properly taxidermist-stuffed, but it didn't look like that great a specimen. Anyway, the thing was huge. It was a wedge-tailed eagle, and I had to get an enormous box filled with foamy material to protect it. I then had to get help carrying it out to the car, and it was a really blustery day, so trying to pick this thing up was difficult. It barely fitted in my car, and I was just thinking that this is the stupidest idea ever.'

Gaby never felt entirely 'embedded' within the Eagles

culture, and in fact 'I felt a little bit intimidated by the blokey culture of the inner football area.' Her favourite coach was Mick Malthouse, 'who I thought was quite nice, although he's loathed in my household, because he turned them into a defensive team. Mind you, with some of the Dockers coaches, my Dockers friends used to tear their hair out. You used to think with the Dockers, "Why don't you get an AFL coach? You know, why not someone with experience?"'

It was a big job for a part-timer, although there were rewards. 'When the club celebrated its tenth anniversary they used one of the albums as part of the promotion on telly, and I remember saying, "Oh, that's my stuff."'

The Eagles ultimately appointed a full-time media person to pick up where Gaby left off, as archivist. She'd been given season tickets for the duration of her time there, for which she was grateful. The derby games are difficult for Gaby, mainly because 'for me the Eagles are my first team but the Dockers are my second. But for some of my Dockers friends, the Eagles are definitely *not* their second. I mean, of the people I know who followed WAFL football, those who followed the two strong Fremantle teams were very passionate. And I can't imagine driving into Freo on a big derby day and seeing any Eagles balloons out. It's become bigger than it used to be, that rivalry, and there seems to be a real divide between port and city. For example, in Tim Winton's novel *Eyrie*, there's a real sense of divide in that book. So I think it's coming out in a lot of things beside football.' The fact that both teams are competitive has added spice to the derby rivalry, and Gaby prefers 'a close game because it's better to watch, as long as the Eagles win of course.'

Gaby is not the only Eagles fan to barrack for the Dockers as her second team, because it's 'us against the Eastern States. I think a lot of Eagles fans really want to see Freo doing well.' The best and funniest example that Gaby comes up with to describe such a fan, is that of an elderly lady who sat a few rows in front of her at Eagles home games. 'She obviously did a lot of her own knitting, because she had her own knitted Eagles scarf, and Eagles beanie, and a little knitted blanket in Eagles colours. And then I went to a Dockers home derby, and she was in the same seat, with the same knitted scarf, beanie and blanket, but they were all in Dockers colours. So she'd knitted herself a twin-set, and I thought it was hilarious.'

MELISSA PARKE – DOCKERS

Melissa Parke is the recently retired federal member of parliament for the seat of Fremantle. It's always been a safe Labor seat, often considered the jewel in the Labor crown, producing a number of ministers and one prime minister. Melissa served in the House of Representatives from 2007 to 2016, during which time she was made minister for International Development. During her time in parliament she was the definition of a conviction politician, and often took positions contrary to her party's official policy. Prior to that Melissa worked as a lawyer for the United Nations, in war zones such as Gaza, Lebanon and Kosovo, and before that she was solicitor-in-charge at the Bunbury Community Legal Centre. Because they're Western Australian, Melissa thinks of the West Coast Eagles as her second team, although her support for the Fremantle Dockers has a political and social dimension that doesn't apply to the Eagles.

Melissa grew up on an apple farm in Donnybrook, where football 'was very much a part of my family life. My great-uncle George was a well-known member of the Donnybrook football team. As well as his playing football, I've always been told that George was well known for not wearing socks. He never wore socks, whether he was playing or not. And my dad and brothers played, so I grew up going to the games. I loved the 1977 grand final, when Donnybrook played South Bunbury, and which Donnybrook won when South Bunbury was the big team down there. It was a big deal to beat them at Hands Oval, especially since it was the first time Donnybrook had won a grand final since the club was formed in 1897. And there's a nice bit of synchronicity there with the Fremantle WAFL teams, because Donnybrook's colours were blue and white, and South Bunbury's were red and white. If you mix those colours, red and blue together, you get Dockers purple.'

Melissa kicked the footy around with her brothers, and still enjoys having a kick now. 'My husband, Warwick, and I like to take our bikes and ride to the park and have a kick of the footy.'

Melissa grew up supporting South Fremantle, following her father's team. 'He's a farmer, but for a while he was a police cadet in Perth, and he used to come to South Freo games. He was always regaling me with stories about John Todd and John Gerovich, and of course Jack Sheedy, so I feel following Freo is very much a part of me. Football to me is all about community and team spirit, and Fremantle's like a big country town – it has the same atmosphere being here supporting the Dockers as it did being part of the community in Donnybrook supporting the Donnybrook Football Club.'

There's the keeping of her father's allegiance to Fremantle, but there's more to it than that. 'The West Coast have always had elitist connotations, a little bit western suburbs, whereas the Fremantle Dockers come out of a working-class community associated with hard work and social justice and struggle, the same spirit that the maritime workers have always shown. The Dockers maintain that tradition very well, if you look at their community work, particularly in the area of Indigenous engagement and development. The club's been very involved in projects to improve mental health especially for Indigenous people.'

Saying that, Melissa has gone to great lengths to support the Eagles on occasions. While working for the UN in New

York, she caught the 2005 grand final between the Eagles and Sydney in a Times Square sports bar in the middle of the night, surrounded by fellow Australians, and watching the game gave her 'a great sense of pride.' The following year's grand final was a more challenging proposition, albeit rewarding when the Eagles won. 'That year I was based in Lebanon, and we were evacuated to Cyprus when the war began between Israel and Hezbollah. I watched the grand final at the UN-peacekeeping base with three other Australians, from the Australian Federal Police. Two of them were supporting Sydney, and there was one guy supporting West Coast with me. The West Coast won, and I was so happy for them. Of course, since leaving the UN and moving back to Fremantle, I've become pretty much a one-eyed Dockers supporter, although if West Coast got into a grand final and Fremantle didn't, like in 2015, I still hoped they would win.'

Asked whether, if the Fremantle Dockers clearly exhibit Labor values, then the opposite applies to the Eagles, Melissa laughs. 'Well, Julie Bishop is a very, very strong Eagles supporter!' Former Western Australian premier and Member for Fremantle Carmen Lawrence was the inaugural Dockers number-one ticket holder between 1995 and 1996, and Melissa would 'have loved nothing more than to be the number-one ticket holder, but sadly it wasn't to be. I guess they didn't want to alienate people who voted for the other side.'

Whatever the political persuasion, being a federal politician involves long hours and plenty of time away from home. In Canberra, following the football meant participating in the press gallery tipping competition. Describing an experience familiar to many Dockers supporters during their less successful years, Melissa 'always tipped the Dockers to win, and one year won the prize for being at the bottom. I received a carton of Little Creatures beer as the consolation prize for coming last, but you know, that was due to loyalty. Parliament was divided because there are the rugby states and the AFL states, and there's almost no crossover. Ken Wyatt [Liberal Member for Hasluck] was a good Dockers supporter.' One person Melissa misses from the press gallery, and a writer on all things Dockers who she used to read while posted overseas with the UN, is journalist Matt Price, who died young in 2007. Price was a writer who understood the absurd drama and sometimes comic aspects and the tenacity of those years when the Dockers struggled to win a game, and who later famously dedicated a whole chapter to Clive Waterhouse in his book *Way to Go: Sadness, Euphoria and the Fremantle Dockers*. 'I only met him the one time when I was first running for parliament, out on the campaign trail. We just walked along talking about the Dockers, and when he died a little later there was a gaping hole in the press gallery, and in the literature of writing about the game, and it's so sad that he's not there anymore.'

Watching Dockers games has taught Melissa something about herself. 'It's been such a hard slog for Fremantle, and it feels like we have the underdog status even when we're high up on the ladder. We weren't given anything on a silver platter, and we've had to earn it. I'm usually someone who supports the underdog, and that's why I've chosen the careers I have, but I must say that when I'm watching Fremantle play, I just want them to win and I don't care about the other side, or how sad they are about it. Watching the games is obviously exciting, but it can also be stressful. If the game is going horribly wrong, I might go and do something else for a bit, and then come back. Sometimes you can't help calling out "Damn!" or (to someone on the other side) "You bastard!" or things like that, although I don't support name-calling, at least not *loudly*.'

Melissa's favourite players over the years illustrate the values she ascribes to the team culture in general. 'I loved Matthew Pavlich, because he was not only such a brilliant player, he was also a wonderful person – a warm and ethical person. He was such a good role model for the younger players. I also love Michael Johnson and Michael Walters, who are gorgeous guys as well. I appreciate all of the players, but those three epitomise what I like about the Dockers – their spirit and tenacity but also their humility. They're not boasters – they're very modest.'

Build-ups to important games like the derby weeks involved Melissa mentioning her Dockers allegiance in speeches. 'I always try to get an assessment of how many Dockers supporters there are in the audience. I also wear purple. Purple earrings, a necklace with an anchor, and a purple scarf. I recently attended the opening of the ballet *Coppelia* at His Majesty's, and I deliberately wore my purple scarf in defiance of the ballet set, who I thought were probably mostly Eagles supporters. I love the colour purple anyway, so all in all, I'm very happy that the Dockers' colour is purple.'

Asked to comment on that anomalous feature of Australian Rules – namely that, of all the world's sporting codes played by men, footy alone has a majority female fan base – Melissa's answer speaks to both the nature of the game and its social history that, for her, is also an aspect of personal history. 'It's not like cricket, which lots of women find tedious, although personally I like cricket. And it's not like rugby, which is an incredibly boring game for spectators – all stop-start, stop-start, stop-start. Footy is a free-running, fast-paced game. And many women grew up watching it and got hooked on it. And like me, many women grew up kicking the footy around, which is something that I still like to do.'

JULIE BISHOP – EAGLES

Framed by the dim light entering the Japanese-style garden behind her, Julie Bishop looks every bit the shrewd negotiator that's made her such an effective foreign minister during the tenure of the Liberal National Party government. She smiles, and wants to know which team we support: Dockers or Eagles. We're in her Subiaco offices, and over her shoulder within the indoor/outdoor garden sits the famous garden gnome. Invited onto The Chaser's election coverage, *Yes We Canberra!* to test her Death Stare on national television, Bishop bested the gnome, which inexplicably toppled off the table and broke. The Chaser boys gifted her the vanquished gnome, and it lives now in her garden, as trophy and reminder. If you can beat a ceramic garden gnome in a staring competition, then presumably hyper-masculine types like Vladimir Putin hold no fear.

Before Julie Bishop was deputy leader of the Liberal Party, and Minister for Foreign Affairs, she was elected as the MP for Curtin, a western-suburbs federal seat that she's held for the LNP since 1998, and which the Libs have held since 1949. She moved to Perth from Adelaide in 1983, working as a lawyer and then managing partner of the firm. She'd grown up on a farm in the Adelaide Hills of cherry and apple orchards, where they also raised sheep. Her father played football for Forest Range, whose colours were red and white, leading Julie to choose North Adelaide as her favourite team in the SANFL. It was very much a football household, with her grandmother following Sturt, and Julie going to football games with her father.

When Julie moved to Perth, she lived in Claremont, and later Subiaco. She naturally began following Claremont in the WAFL league, but because of her SANFL allegiance the local league never really captured her attention. It was only when the Eagles came along in 1987 that she became 'really excited, because now there was a team that could embrace all of that rivalry between South Australian teams and Victorian teams, and to have a team from West Australia actually playing against the Victorians appealed to me a great deal.' If the Eagles were initially a proxy vehicle to channel the traditional antipathy towards Victorian football, common to both Western Australia and South Australian football leagues, Julie's embracing of the West Coast Eagles also had to do with her early involvement in the development of the club. 'My law firm did the legal work for the establishment of the West Coast Eagles, and so the whole concept of having a state team out of Western Australia, in a national competition, was exciting. I was inspired to get behind this new club, because I really thought it could make a difference to the AFL.'

When the Adelaide Crows entered the league shortly after, Julie wasn't tempted. 'I lived just up the road from Subiaco Oval, and I was making my life here. It was also an exciting time to be in the West. I decided I was going to stay in Perth, so there was no question of going back to Adelaide or supporting the Crows, although my dad follows the Crows religiously. He follows it intensely, especially when the Eagles are playing the Crows – he just loves his football. I took him to an Eagles–Crows game in Adelaide a couple of years ago, and he loved it.'

The Eagles were an exciting team 'because we were all starting afresh. I went to the grand final against Hawthorn in 1991, and that was a sad day, but I also went to the following year's grand final when we won. I also went to the 2005 grand final when we lost, and in 2006 when we won. I was of course there in 2015 when again we lost, and I was sure we'd win in 2016.'

Being a federal MP means plenty of time on the road, but also the opportunity to see the Eagles play in Melbourne. Since taking on the Minister for Foreign Affairs portfolio, however, 'I tend to be overseas on weekends. But I still follow the football absolutely. I follow the games on Twitter and I retweet wherever I am in the world. I've got a photograph of myself and my media adviser, Gaby, during the 2015 preliminary final against Hawthorn, when we were in New York for the UN General Assembly leaders week. We got the game up on my iPad and we watched it, and I tweeted the photograph of us wearing our Eagles scarves watching the game.' Back in Canberra, there is friendly rivalry to be had. Fellow West Australian LNP Member for Hasluck, Ken Wyatt, is a keen Dockers fan, and 'Ken sits in the front in partyroom meetings. We have partyroom meetings in Canberra every Tuesday when parliament's sitting, and as part of the leadership group I sit facing the backbench, and Ken sits in the front row, facing me. And there have been times when I'll bring in an Eagles scarf and just throw it on the table, or he'll walk in with a Dockers scarf, or he'll bring in his Dockers mug to drink coffee in front of me, and we do tease each other a lot.'

Julie's favourite players over the years include John Worsfold, who she 'got to know when I was on the board of the club. He was such a dominant figure both as a player and a coach, and I've always admired the role he played at the Eagles from early on. I was a big fan of Chris Judd when he was captain and I thought he was superb. And I've always enjoyed watching Ben Cousins – he is *beautiful* to watch.'

The derby rivalry between the two WA teams is also something that Julie keenly enjoys. 'I think the rivalry between the Eagles and the Dockers is now legendary. It's one of the great competitions in Australian sport, and the derbies are always played like grand finals, which I think makes our teams even better for taking on the Victorians. When the Eagles and the Dockers play, it has all the brutality and the intensity of some of the fiercest games played in the AFL. That Demolition Derby in 2000 – I don't think I've ever seen anything like it. We've never had a drawn derby, but we've had two decided by a point. Derbies just have that intensity – it's like family playing family.'

Asked to name her favourite derby, Julie comes down on the side of the second derby in 2015. 'That game resonated for me because we were up for a challenge, and because we had so many injured. We won by twenty-four points, and I thought that was pretty magical. It meant a lot to me, because it meant that we were in with a chance in the grand final. We were both first and second on the ladder, and it made me appreciate how far Western Australian football has come. At that moment, I think that our football came of age, and it sent a really powerful message across the country that the Eagles were a team to be reckoned with.'

The idea of a derby grand final appeals to Julie as another demonstration of how far Western Australian football has come, and its potential annoyance value to Victorian teams. 'I remember when we played Hawthorn in 1991. The Victorians were outraged that a non-Victorian team was playing in the grand final. And then the same in 2005 and 2006, when the Eagles and Sydney played, and the media kept making it up that Sydney was really South Melbourne. They just couldn't handle it, and I can't wait for a derby grand final. Working on the assumption that the Eagles won it on the first time around, the Dockers would be working very hard to repeat the occasion, so that they could knock us off.'

When a derby grand final was looking possible in 2015, Julie rather cheekily took the microphone off a nearby journalist and put the question to AFL CEO Gillon McLaughlin after his speech at the National Press Club in Canberra, as to where a derby Grand Final might be fixtured. Implicit in the question was that it should be held in Western Australia, but McLaughlin's response was to apologetically acknowledge the MCG's contractual right to hold grand finals until 2038.

It's not the first time that Julie Bishop has astutely advanced the interests of her club by way of her official role. There is a framed photograph in her office of another such occasion that Julie and the Eagles later tweeted. 'When we were in opposition I was invited to meet with President Obama, and of course there's very strict security around the President. You're not allowed to take in mobile phones, or cameras, or anything like that, but I wanted to give him a gift. So I folded up an Eagles jumper to make it look like a little purse, a little cloth purse, and when I walked up to him, at the moment the official photographer went to take our photo, I unrolled it and it was an Eagles guernsey. I explained that the Eagles were like the Pittsburgh Steelers, because I knew that was his team, and he took it with very good grace. And of course the Eagles were very keen on the photograph, and that photo, it went viral. I just love my footy and the Eagles, and I'd no sooner leave them than fly to the moon.'

PARSI – EAGLES

Parsi is an Eagles supporter who moved to Fremantle in 1983, and has lived there ever since. He was part of the port city's dynamic sannyasin community, which is often considered to be largely responsible for kickstarting Fremantle's renovation boom. Parsi works in the area of Aboriginal workforce development, getting Indigenous people into employment, but back then he was involved with winding down the Orange People's assets in Fremantle – properties and businesses and schools – following the closure of their communes in India and the United States.

Parsi grew up in Bassendean, although he barracked for East Perth in the WAFL, following in his father's footsteps. His mother, however, was a staunch West Perth supporter, because her father had been secretary of the West Perth Football Club for a decade, and had managed a couple of state teams that travelled to South Australia in the 1930s. Derby rivalry is something that Parsi grew up with, because it was 'like that in my family. We'd always go to the East Perth–West Perth derby games together and my grandfather would be so feisty, and he'd end up having vocal arguments with people and he was mad for it, so I grew up with that passion. It was all pretty intense, and East Perth was a tough area in those days. When there were finals, we used to go to Subiaco Oval the night before, and everybody would camp out, so there would be thousands of people camping out overnight and it was all great fun.'

Parsi played footy as a junior for Ashfield, Stan Nowotny

and Wayne Otway's old club, and he also completed a preseason with Swan Districts in 1970. 'I did nearly all the preseason. Bill Walker was the coach, which was fantastic. We did some long runs through national parks and one run we did – I think there were one hundred and eight of us – we did through the John Forrest National Park and it was an incredible run. I think it was eleven miles (it felt like a thousand), on bush tracks, and it was stinking hot, and I remember noticing how Bill Walker was so fit. You'd be going up these hills, and the only way you knew where the track was, was by the tape they'd attached to trees, and you'd get to the top of a hill and hear guys vomiting in the valley below, and Bill would run down and spur them on, and then come past you again; he was unreal. He looked as fresh at the end as he did when he started. It was quite inspiring to see and you realised how dedicated he was. We got to the railway spur that was the end of the course, and I came in fortieth or thereabouts and it was all just blue metal and we were literally crawling towards the end, and the trainers who were waiting for us lowered us into the pool that was there. Unfortunately, we then moved on to training at the Bassendean Oval. I lived pretty close to there, and there was a superphosphate plant just up the road, and I had chronic bronchial asthma. The plant used to blow its stacks two or three times a week, and this cloud would drift across the whole suburb, and unfortunately I was doing sprint training when this happened and I had an asthma attack, and ended up in hospital. But all my good mates were at the Swans, and some older boys who ended up playing two hundred games and that for the Swans – local guys like Tommy Mullooly and Steve Gillespie from the Bassendean Junior Football Club. Greg Latham and Laurie Andrew were schoolmates who were playing league and reserves for Swans while still doing their Leaving at Cyril Jackson High School – I reckon we had the best ruck division of any high school in the state. I went over to the Bayswater Amateur Football Club, the Bulldogs, which was a very old and proud club that I was very proud to play for. I ended up being captain one year, and won a fairest and best and best on ground in a grand final, although I had to stop when I was twenty because I had too many concussions.'

Parsi ended up 'running hotels for many years' and played a single game for Broome Towns Football Club when he was thirty against an all-Aboriginal team in Broome and 'it was hilarious, because I'm this old white guy and all the kids are twenty, and they were just going past me like billyo, you know. I remember my last kick in footy was a goal and that was just because they'd forgotten about me, I was so slow. There are many wonderfully talented players in that competition.' Not long after he kicked the goal, Parsi was bouncing the ball down a wing when he stepped into a hole, where someone had left off the sprinkler irrigation lid, and ended up with his leg in a cast for several months.

Parsi considers himself a Freo person, and Fremantle his home. He became an Eagles supporter when they first came into the competition, because it was 'WA versus the Vics and I thought great, let's give it to 'em, although it was pretty funny because I am part of the Orange People community, and footy passion and following a guru don't really go hand in hand. Gurus are not really into contact sports, and they tend to be a bit cynical about that kind of thing. It was quite interesting, because you'd have some of us Australians doing meditations and all that, and then we'd turn into rabid football followers.'

When the Dockers came on the scene, plenty of Freo people Parsi knew were ready to switch allegiances. 'My life and my community was in the Fremantle district, but I was an Eagles supporter, and I stayed the course, you know. Of course there was right away a great divide, and fierce rivalry, and a lot of shenanigans about who was going to be on which side, and of course we fiercely tried to recruit people from one team to another. It took a couple of years, and there were a couple of ladies who were a bit ambivalent, but after getting a few membership applications in the mail we convinced them to follow the Eagles. But as soon as it was announced that there would be a Fremantle side, there were people saying, "I'm with Fremantle," and so even before Fremantle were a club the battlelines had been formed. And then the banter started: "You wait till we get a club there, then we're going to kick your so-and-so."'

But Parsi has some sympathy for the Dockers too. 'When Fremantle started, they got a raw deal from the AFL, an absolutely disgraceful deal in terms of the way the funding was done, and the draft picks and the infrastructure. They were very lucky that they got a good leader like Ben Allan to come along. I'm still of the opinion that it's not the AFL, but that it's still the VFL, and they were very afraid of Western Australian dominance, and made sure that the Dockers were hard done by. I'm a very strong Eagles supporter, but I love watching Fremantle play – I really like what they're doing at the moment. When I have Aboriginal kids come down from the country to study, wherever I can, I take them down to the Dockers training at Fremantle Oval to get autographs, and they just love it. There's always been a lot of great Aboriginal men play for Freo, and I think that's a big plus for the club, and the Aboriginal community.'

Derby day in Fremantle for Parsi's community is always special. Right from the first derby, the footy fans used to gather in numbers at a Freo house and 'although we'd be divided, we'd all get together to watch the game. We'd all be in our colours, and there'd be twenty or thirty people in the room, all shouting, and it was just going off, and bragging rights were fiercely contested. We won the first nine derbies, of course, but you know, you get your licks in while you can.'

Parsi's most memorable derby was actually an Eagles loss, on the occasion of the first Dockers derby win in 1999. Parsi watched the game at the usual place in Fremantle, and after the siren sounded, and the post-mortem discussion had been done, Parsi got into his car to drive home. 'But I had an Eagles sticker on my car – on the bumper and rear window. And of course you could hear all over Freo people screaming, horns tooting and klaxons going, and anyway I started driving away from my mate's place to head back to South Fremantle, and I didn't get very far before I realised I had a convoy behind me, because they were all following me because of my Eagles stickers. And they're tooting, and it started with about five cars, and everywhere the roads were just full of Dockers fans. So I turned right and drove right through Freo, and of course the convoy kept getting bigger and bigger, until there were about twenty cars, and I drove out over the bridges, and they kept tooting and waving their flags, and they followed me back and they were just ecstatic you know, they were deliriously happy. There I was just peacefully driving home, and I look in the mirror and there's these mad fans following me everywhere and it was very funny.'

Parsi would welcome a derby grand final, 'although it would be brutal – it would be last man standing, but absolutely fantastic. You've got to be in it to win it, and it'd be bragging rights forever, and what a great thing for WA footy.'

Were a derby grand final to eventuate, as a Freo person, and after his last experience of a Dockers grand final, Parsi knows where he'll be. 'We watched the 2013 Dockers grand final loss at a friend's house, and had a few drinks and carried on, and we were really very disappointed when the Dockers lost. There was a whole pile of us, and so we walked into Fremantle after the game, and there in central Freo was one of the most amazing things I've ever seen. Even though Freo had lost, it was like the Carnival in Rio, it was just huge. It was one of the most amazing parties I've ever experienced, and there were literally thousands upon thousands of people – you could not move on the streets, it was that crowded, and we just wanted to go and be in it. Fremantle: it's the Dockers' and my spiritual home.'

IAN MACRAE – EAGLES

Many are called, but few are chosen. At least that's how real estate agent Ian MacRae felt, when he finally accepted that his football talents weren't going to take him into the big league. The son of a Scottish migrant, Ian grew up in Scarborough. His dad was a Glasgow Rangers fan back in the old country, and soon adopted the corresponding blue and white of East Fremantle. Ian was initially drawn to Claremont, but had a conversion experience in church one day that switched him to West Perth. 'Standing in front of me one Sunday was this huge man with flaming red hair. I asked Dad who it was, and he told me it was Blue Foley, who played for West Perth. Blue had my attention, and from that moment on I was a Cardie.'

Ian's parents became Cardinals fans too, and going to the matches against archenemies East Perth was a nice 'introduction to the religion of football' and more importantly into the fierce rivalry of the derby. Ian played schoolboy football but soon recognised that 'my aspirations far outweighed my ability. I was never going to be the footballer I wanted to be, and so I became interested in coaching techniques. I remember sitting at Leederville Oval one reserves match, and Clinton Farmer, the ex–East Fremantle rover, was coaching. Dennis Cometti was the league coach, and both of them were very innovative in their day. Farmer was the first coach that I'd ever seen who pushed an entire backline up to the forward line, and then concertinaed back again when the ball was retreating. It was clever but it didn't last for long – in retrospect, the players didn't have the fitness they do now to maintain it all day.'

At this time Ian was involved in his first career of teaching. He was at Trinity College, coaching the primary-school team, and was approached to ask if he'd coach the high-school team. 'We had a very successful first year [1987] and won the CIG Cup. We beat Hamilton Hill High, who at that stage had a young South Fremantle colts player called Glen Jakovich.'

The win caught the attention of WAFL development officer, Grant Dorrington, who called Ian the following Monday, and asked if he'd take the role of assistant coach for the Teal Cup team. Ian coached and worked as a selector for the state schoolboy team for a period of eight years. When fellow Teal Cup selector Michael Moylan was appointed as an Eagles selector, Ian was approached to join West Coast as a talent scout. 'I must've made a couple of selections which tickled Michael's fancy, because in 1989 I was asked if I could recruit for the Eagles, primarily focusing on private schoolboys, because at that point the club considered that the best junior players came from the private school system. So there was myself, Mick Moylan, Noel Carter, the late Geoffrey Christian and Trevor Woodhouse. I was already a West Coast supporter, but that was when my passion got developed further. I brought the knowledge of all these young schoolboy footballers.'

Recruiting from the draft in the early days of the Eagles was slightly different to now, when the team might be expected to take the best talent available, rather than draft a player to fill a specific role. Drew Banfield was Ian's first 'number-one draft pick' recruit, then playing amateurs rather than WAFL. While Banfield wasn't 'the entire package', he was drafted specifically to replace Dwayne

'Fat' Lamb, going on to play more than two hundred games and help the Eagles win a premiership. The culture at the Eagles, under Nesbitt, was all about excellence and loyalty, and was 'modelled unashamedly on Hawthorn.' Nesbitt's approach was that you were 'either with the club or not with the club', and so when the Dockers joined the AFL, there was no chance that Ian would entertain becoming a fan, although more broadly he thought that 'it was a wonderful opportunity to have something that was missing from local AFL football in Perth, and that is rivalry.'

But there was a huge cultural and financial gap between the two clubs. 'I thought Fremantle started with all guns blazing, but they were scatterguns. They were put together by the Claremont WAFL hierarchy, and that's natural for a coach who's unfamiliar with the AFL. For example, I received a call from Peter Bell one day, who wanted to meet me about something urgent. I asked him what the problem was, and he said that he'd just gone down to Dockers training, and that Gerard McNeil had thrust a jumper on him in front of a Channel Nine television camera. The reporter had said, "How does it feel to be the Dockers' first signing?" And Peter told me that he hadn't signed anything. So I rang up Micky Moylan, and we made a dot-point list of things that should happen regarding Peter's HECS fees, his medical fees, et cetera. So in a sense, the Eagles scripted Peter Bell's first contract with the Dockers, and I thought gee, that's really B-grade. And it put Belly on the wrong foot with the club, and unfortunately he also got on the wrong foot with the coach that year.'

The idea that the Eagles had it easy in comparison with the Dockers is something that rankles with Ian. 'It's a myth. We started with a list of thirty-five, that's ten fewer players than the Dockers' first list, and you know we didn't receive the first selection of the best WA players. We had no template to work from either. You know, they started out training out at Guildford Oval.'

Ian was present at the first derby, and understood that the first five years of derby losses would 'leave a scar on the Dockers' psyche. Although, out of the furnace of continual failure, has come a reward. Because I was with the recruiting staff, I was at that first derby, and it began with Johnny Worsfold running up to Winston Abraham before the first bounce. And he was poking Abraham in the chest, almost forcing his fingers through Abraham's ribcage, repeating the same thing, and you could see it took Abraham by surprise. Worsfold's face had that glazed look he got when he crossed the white line, and anyway, I couldn't wait to find out what he'd been saying to Abraham. And I found out he was just repeating the line, "The coach says I get to play on you. I get to play on *you*. I get to play on *you*." So it was the Eagles as a playing group, drawing a line in the sand and saying, "We're the big boys, *bang*!" And I thought, "That was a statement, and it's going to create a terrific rivalry here." Some of the Dockers players weren't eighty-five kilos if they were wet in the shower, and our players, well, it was a thing in the early '90s that players needed bulk to survive.'

Ian's favourite Eagles players in derbies include the 'blissfully skilful Dean Kemp. One of the greatest players out of WA. If it wasn't for the fact that his head was used as a barge-board so often, he would've played three hundred games. And of course Peter Matera. I remember taking a chap over from America to a game at Subiaco Oval. It was his first AFL game, and at some point he asked me, "Who's that guy there?" And I said, "Peter Matera, why do you ask?" and he said, "He plays it differently to everyone else," and I thought, "How beautifully put."'

One other player Ian remembers in the schoolboy league was a young Nat Fyfe, playing for Aquinas against

Christchurch. 'I left teaching ten years ago, but I occasionally watch games, and called Serge Miller at the Eagles and said, "Hey, you've got to have a look at this bloke." I went along to a game to watch someone else I had my eye on as a potential recruit, but what caught my eye was this skinny kid, and I mean skinny as *skinny*. He did a corkscrew in the air and took a mark and hit the ground and went off running and I thought, "God, that was unique." And now he's out there, flying across the packs like Royce Hart.'

One of Ian's proudest achievements was bringing a then Aquinas schoolboy to the notice of Teal Cup selectors. Ian was watching an interschool year nine game down on Memorial Oval. The deal was that Aquinas ask a boarder to stand behind the goals to retrieve the ball if there was a score – to get the ball back on the field more quickly and keep up the momentum (although when the opposition scored they had to fetch the ball themselves). 'Anyway, I'm sitting down and there's this little midget behind goals doubling as a goal umpire. And I'm jotting down some notes after a goal has been scored, and the ball's been beautifully kicked back from the goals into the centre square. So I thought, "Who kicked that?" But there was just this little kid. Anyway, another goal was scored and I watched this time, and the kid let go – another barrel – and I'd say it was a good fifty metres. You know, a decent wallop for a little kid, and at the end of the match I went and introduced myself. I asked him where he'd played football last year and he said Kojonup A's. And I'm thinking Kojonup under-15 A's, and I asked him how the season went, and he replied, "Oh, I didn't play the whole season. I broke my leg in a game, and my dad won't let me play against the men anymore." And I said, "*Sorry*, against the men?" He was playing in the country league A-grade competition as a fourteen-year-old, and not a big fourteen-year-old either. I knew the State Schoolboys team was leaving for interstate, so I went and watched the kid play, and called up the Teal Cup selector, and told him that I'd found him a rover. I told him that I'd seen the kid play, and that he played a different game to everyone else on the field. The selector took my word for it, and the next thing the kid's gone across playing for the state team, and in his first match he got thirty-one possessions, and in his second match he was tagged.'

And that, right there, 'is how the story of Peter Bell started.'

ALISON FAN – DOCKERS

You'd have to walk a long way to find a more passionate Dockers supporter than Alison Fan, although she insists that her American husband, Duncan, who painted the giant picture of Luke McPharlin taking a classic hang during a derby game, up there on the living-room wall, is even more fanatical. They live in Nedlands, deep in the heartland of what many consider to be prime Eagles territory, and the feeling of being besieged is certainly evident.

Alison Fan is a very well-known journalist who has worked in the Western Australian media as a reporter, columnist and television newsreader for some five decades. In 1989, fifty-five of the sixty-eight kilograms heisted in the Perth Mint Swindle was returned as gold pellets, seven years after the original theft. And it was delivered to Alison Fan, then working with Channel Seven, along with a note protesting the Mickelberg brothers' innocence.

Now 'closer to seventy than she is to sixty', Alison's introduction to football came as a teenager when she was briefly engaged to legendary full-forward Austin Robertson junior (still a family friend and Dockers supporter). Her interest in the game way back then was marginal, 'I was only really interested in clothes and parties.' It was only when she returned from the US with her husband, an avid New York Jets and Yankees fan who was introduced to Subiaco football by Austin, that she resumed going to the games. 'An experience that probably prepared us for being Dockers supporters, because Subiaco hadn't won a grand final in ages.

There was a famous prophecy made back in the '40s that 'man would walk on the moon before Subiaco wins a premiership', and that's what happened – Subiaco didn't win a grand final until 1973.'

When the Eagles were born, Alison and Duncan became supporters and 'it was more of a social outing because all of our close friends are Eagles and they used to say, "Oh, you're so objective," but of course it's easy to be objective when you don't care about the outcome. I became a Dockers fan, but it was only during our very first derby that I turned into this irrational one-eyed fanatic. I don't know if it was because we were the underdogs and lost the game, but by the end of it I felt like punching out every Eagles supporter in sight.

'It also became a personal thing. At work I was next to Chris Mainwaring, Adrian Barich, and Jeff Newman. And though I love Jeff to bits, he was always putting these Eagles membership forms on my desk saying, "Come back." Even my hairdresser Maurice Meade was querying how I had become a "traitor"; they actually used that word.'

Alison finds it difficult to explain that passion to non-football followers, and in particular how she delays responding to social invitations if they clash with football.

'How do you explain to a non-believer that you have been up all night before a game thinking maybe they should move Pav into half-back and Ballas into the centre? There are doodling scribbles all over the house with arrows and players' names after we both analyse, agonise, and argue over positions and passages of play.'

Over the past twenty years Alison has been asked to join various Freo committees but she has always resisted because that means 'turning a passion into a job.'

And though denying she is superstitious, she admits to wearing certain purple socks and a particular scarf to each game, and throwing out other purple items after a particularly bad defeat. 'I knew it was those purple boots that brought bad luck. It's some inherent tribal thing – how else do you explain it?'

Alison and Duncan have been there from the start, 'right through all those horrible years when they were being demolished week after week. We were that clichéd, we'd start off in denial, then anger after the game, and by midweek it was acceptance.'

As for the players, Alison has great memories of Jeff Farmer, and she has walked the talk. When working as a court reporter, and Farmer was due to appear on one of his misdemeanours, Alison tagged him into the court with his lawyer, John Prior. 'I said to Jeff, "I'll walk in with you. Don't react to the yahoos yelling things, the cameras are all on you. Don't smile. Don't smile." Then when some guy yelled out, "You dickhead, you should go to jail," I just repeated, "keep walking, don't turn around, keep going." The following week I sent him a best-of-luck card and it became a sort of tradition before games.

'When I quit Channel Seven News to go part-time with *Today Tonight*, there was a bit of publicity and Jeff arrived suddenly at our front door with a bunch of red roses – bigger than him. He was so sweet and nice, and remains one of our most exciting players of all time.'

The only other time Alison has written to a player was after one of the most spiteful derby games on record (though she has not been shy at penning her thoughts to various CEOs at Fremantle).

'It was a kind of supporter letter to Steven Dodd after he was suspended for what Duncan described as a perfect right hook. In hindsight, as a grandmother, I can say it was probably not a politically correct thing to do.

But derby games do bring out the best ... and worst. 'I think it's all about ego and pride because I was only sulky and nasty when we lost all those derbies. I realised that after we started winning derby after derby – I became quite ambivalent. But I will still never go to an Eagles home game or derby because I don't trust my behaviour. And Duncan says he doesn't want to have to step in and defend me.

'Derby games take you to another level and certainly raise the adrenaline. I remember turning off the TV midway through a game when the Eagles were killing us and going out to hand-plane an old wooden dresser. It was only when splinters start to fly off I realised I had gone through three coats of paint and taken off the actual real wood – all during half-time.'

Alison doesn't see it as a bad thing that Fremantle's team culture has become more ruthless, something exemplified by the firing of coach Mark Harvey in 2011, and the subsequent hiring of Ross Lyon.

'I love Ross Lyon and what he's brought to the game. Eagles friends have always said Fremantle's culture was too laidback and too accepting. And they were probably right, especially in the early years. My job as a news journo has always been to play hardball with no excuses and to win. And I expect the same from professional footballers. Having said that, why do we still hang in there year after year? It's an inexplicable phenomenon.'

And as they say, there's always next year.

An annual ritual for Alison is to book grand final airfares before the season even starts. This optimism began in 1995, the Dockers' very first season, when she packed warm footy clothes for a humid September Singapore holiday – just in case the Dockers made the finals and she'd need to fly into a Melbourne winter.

Alison admits to 'getting a really flat feeling when footy season finishes,' although there's always a visible reminder of the grace and beauty of the game on their living-room wall, in the form of Duncan's painting of Luke McPharlin's official Mark of the Year in 2005. 'Over the Eagles of course.'

It's an iconic grab with McPharlin soaring above team mate Josh Carr to take the ball on his chest, impossibly high, but as Alison points out, wearing an expression of 'improbable and perfect calm.'

JAMES BAKER – EAGLES

When James Baker celebrated his sixtieth birthday, he did it in full rock'n'roll style, playing a gig at Mojos with his current band, The Painkillers. They also played at his wedding reception, along with other bands whose members include luminaries from Perth's punk and rock scene dating back some four decades. James Baker is rock royalty, and some of the bands he's played in are some of Australia's most influential and canonical – think The Victims, The Scientists, Hoodoo Gurus, Beasts of Bourbon and The Dubrovniks. The Rockin Hendy and The Painkillers, consisting of James, Richard Lane from The Stems, Josh Reynolds aka Joe Bludge, and Bad Seeds' and ex-Triffids' bassist Martyn P. Casey, still play around Perth and always pull a crowd.

We meet James and his wife Cathy at Shark Park, the home of the East Fremantle Football Club, and not more than a few hundred metres from where James grew up, on Marmion Street. His father played reserves for the Old Easts, and his mother was a mad-keen South Fremantle supporter. They made sure to take the young James along to every derby game. Even after the family moved to rural Donnybrook for a spell (where James's dad coached the juniors team), they either drove up for the weekend to watch their teams play or listened to it on the wireless. James remembers that on such occasions, 'my dad would be listening to the game on our transistor radio in his armchair in the living room, saying "C'mon East, c'mon East" whilst Mum would be adding "Dirty players, dirty players" as she was supporting South.

This went on each time the two teams played, and although it was serious at the time, it was all in good humour.'

James's family has deep roots in Fremantle, on both his father's and mother's side, which account for the split loyalties between his parents. His grandfather on the Baker side 'was a famous Fremantle guy, and he's still got an award named after him called the Heron Prize at John Curtin High'. (In fact, James' sister's husband was the recipient of this prize in 1968.) James's maternal great-grandfather was a stevedore for Petterson on the Freo wharf, a company that followed Souths. Cathy's family also has roots in the Fremantle area, in that her 'mum's family, one of the Greek families that immigrated to Perth from Kassteloriizo, owned the Richmond Ice Works on The Esplanade, and so I therefore grew up seeing a lot of the stuff that was happening in Freo in the early days of the '60s, '70s and '80s. There's definitely a 'thing' with some of the old people in Fremantle – a culture that goes back to the waterfront and that's really staunch. People have got that thing where they will not cross the line, and I think that's where a lot of the strong emotion around the Dockers–Eagles derby comes from. It's a part of Fremantle's history – it's just got that flavour to it.'

James played footy for Palmyra throughout his childhood, and until he was seventeen. He remembers footy being an important part of his life, 'with my dad teaching me to play kick-to-kick in our backyard, and later on supporting me while playing in club teams on the weekend. I used to sneak onto the East Fremantle ground to kick the footy during the week, and on weekends play on the rocks that used to be around the ground, and watch my heroes like Fred Lewis, Neil Dedman, Bob Johnson, Ray Sorrell, Trizzie Lawrence and Doug Green.'

Football took a back seat when James's music career took off, just after he travelled to the US and Britain in 1976 to see his musical heroes play. 'I was always a rock'n'roll fan and when I got serious about it, I went and lived in America for about six months, and chased down my favourite bands like the Ramones, and the Heartbreakers and Television. They were playing in small clubs and they weren't that famous. I saw the Ramones and the Flamin' Groovies doing a double bill in LA to about a hundred people, and it just blew me away, and I thought there's no way I can go back to the real world, you know. Just after, in London, I was on a double-decker red bus when this guy got on and sat next to me because of my New York Dolls t-shirt. He wasn't called Sid Vicious then but John Ritchie, and he was a nice guy, and occasionally we'd meet and have a beer. One day these skinheads were going to beat me up at a Clash gig and John, who had a bit of a cult following, told them to not touch me and they didn't. So you know, if anyone says anything about Sid Vicious I'm not going to be one to say anything bad about him. I later was invited to audition for The Clash, but I hadn't played for about a year. I later ran into Joe Strummer at a Heartbreakers gig at the Roxy in London and he asked if I would come back and try out again, but I had already booked my passage back to Australia as I was penniless by that time…'

Back in Australia, James's music took him to Sydney, where he used to watch the occasional Sydney game 'because it was a game of footy,' until the West Coast Eagles came along. Both his mother and father started supporting the local team, but it was a personal tragedy that fixed James's loyalty to the Eagles. He was talking to his father about the new team 'and it was just when the West Coast had announced that they were coming into the league, as the first team outside of Victoria. And my dad said to me, "Don't worry, they'll be good." And he died the next day. I was the last person to see my father alive and those were his last words.' After sharing a moment like that with his father, James was never going to support the Dockers when they joined, and neither was his mother, despite their Fremantle histories. When James returned to live in Perth in 1993, he watched the Eagles play night games at the WACA with his mother, having inherited his father's WACA membership. The previous year he'd missed the grand final, while on tour in Europe. 'We were at this hotel in Prague and we got up extremely hungover at six am to watch the game, and the TV had eighteen thousand Sky channels on it, like badminton in England, and baseball in America, and all these other sports, but they didn't have the AFL on and they didn't care less that they didn't have it on. We didn't go on to Holland that day like we were supposed to, and we didn't find out the score for another week.'

James became a regular at Eagles home games, and that had a lot to do with the fact that 'the Eagles were full of East Fremantle players anyway. Mainwaring, Lockyer, Cousins, Kerr, and I just stayed with the Eagles because they were the first local team.'

Saying that, James supports the Eagles first and the Dockers second. 'It pisses me off when Fremantle fans go for the Dockers but hate the Eagles. I still barrack for Fremantle if they're playing anyone else. And I know that the Fremantle supporters call the Eagles chardonnay drinkers, but I think Fremantle members drink more chardonnay and Eagles guys drink more beer. I know you can't generalise, but most Eagles supporters are brickie's-labourer types, and all the Fremantle ones are the yuppies and fans of Eskimo Joe and you know, old hippies.'

James's favourite derby moment was when Hayden Ballantyne missed the shot on goal after the siren in 2011, and the Eagles won by a point. 'It was a great kick from outside fifty, and I thought, you know, good on the man but it hit the post. Most derbies have been great games, and it doesn't bother me that Fremantle has caught up with the West Coast Eagles, because now the derbies are always good, like with East Fremantle and South Fremantle derbies. The way they play they're always equal – no matter which one's on top and which one's on the bottom.'

Both Cathy and James always try to make the WAFL derby between East and South Fremantle whenever possible, because, according to Cathy, 'although James has been really busy with music, there's so many people there involved in the music industry.' Cathy came to football late, having grown up thinking that footy was 'rubbish – just men chasing pigskins around in the mud. And then I went to a game at the MCG in the late '80s. And I said to my friend who was taking me to the MCG, "Oh no, I don't want to go to the bloody football, let's go to an art gallery or something decent," but I got dragged along to this thing and the whole ambience of the place just shifted me, and I thought, "Oh my goodness, there's actually something big going on here." The way the crowd all moved together when the ball moved, and when a goal was kicked and the crowd just roared.'

Cathy and James still go to art galleries, however, and have recently been to the Ramones Museum in Berlin. 'Nearly all of the Ramones stuff is there, they've got Joe's glasses, they've got their shoes and jeans and t-shirts, and you just buy a pint and wander around looking at all this stuff. And bands sometimes go in there and play the venue, it holds about two hundred people. It's bizarre.'

Big games now involve going to James's sister's house in Kelmscott, where pies are the traditional fare, and after picking up his mother, part of the ritual is also that James trims his mother's hedges. It's a source of amusement to him how much football is a part of their relationship. 'I'll phone her up and I'll say, "I'm going on a tour of Europe," and the first thing she'll say is, "Ah, I think the Eagles are going to do well this season." Going to Europe on tour is not as exciting as talking about the Eagles. My mother's just a huge fan, and she'd kill me if I ever switched teams.'

James is happy to move with the times, in that with the trading of his former favourite player Callum Sinclair to the Swans, his new favourite is swapped-in recruit Lewis Jetta, but the conversation moves to a little-known detail about James's drumming, as confided by Cathy. Boogie-woogie and early rock'n'roll might have been inspired by the syncopated rhythm of trains running over tracks, as per the legend, but harking back to his childhood, kicking the footy with his dad in the backyard, for James Baker it's also a fact that he 'has a kick drum on his instrument – for James it's always been about kicking.'

GLEN STASIUK – EAGLES

'There are only two good things to come out of Fremantle. Bon Scott and the Canning Highway.' This is Dr Glen Stasiuk's opening salvo when we meet him at Murdoch University in his cluttered office festooned with books, maps and film ephemera. Glen is a documentary filmmaker, Noongar lecturer and Eagles diehard and he greets us with a t-shirt that reads *I support two teams – the Eagles and anyone who is playing the Dockers.* 'I'm an Eagles supporter because I never had a VFL side. I had mates and a cousin who would follow Carlton because of Peter Bosustow and Kenny Hunter. I did not give a flying duck about any Victorian side – I just loved East Perth.'

Stasiuk recalls going along to Perth Oval and it being very much a family outing. 'I've got some beautiful family memories of sitting behind the Claisebrook end of the ground with my mum, my Aunty Bub (she's a Farmer/Keen) and my nanna (also a Farmer/Keen). We all basically sat behind those goals; wind, rain, hail, shine we were there.' Speaking with Stasiuk, it becomes clear that football literally runs in his veins. He has ancestry with the great Polly Farmer (hence the allegiance to East Perth) and the Haywards, Maley Hayward being one of the early Noongar footballers to play in the WAFL with Claremont in 1928 before moving to South Fremantle. This connection extends into his formative childhood and teenage years and helps explain his deep parochialism. 'I used to love watching *The Winners* and *Countdown*. It was a ritual. On Saturday I'd play and then go and watch East Perth and then on the Sunday I'd watch *The Winners* and watch the great WA players in the VFL. WAFL football was way better than the VFL at that time I reckon.'

Stasiuk regales us with football memories of when he and his mates would wag class at Lynwood High School and head to Subiaco Oval to see the State of Origin games. These games created a strong connection to place and a rivalry that came to mysteriously weave its magic spell on him, in particular on the date of March 29, 1987, when the West Coast Eagles came up against Richmond at Subiaco. He recalls, 'we sat on the hill and just hearing the banter was great. It was standing room. West Coast were a little flashy and weren't playing that well but came back and won the game. I remember young Chris Lewis, Phil Narkle, Alex Ishchenko, Paul Peos (who incidentally had the first ever official kick for the Eagles in that game), Glendinning. I was sold on that first game. I was an Eagles man from that day on.'

For Stasiuk, the journey that the Eagles have taken him on is one that he cherishes, having attended many interstate matches as well as Eagles home games at Subiaco. From these experiences, his favourite Eagles players are some of the most recognisable to have played in the club's history. 'The first of the three best AFL footballers I've seen play and play regularly is Peter Matera. I saw him play at his peak. He's a smart footballer and his nickname, Roo, suits him because that is how he moves, like a *yongka*. That's what Noongars call kangaroos. The other player who is fresh in my memory is Chris Judd. I saw Chris Judd do stuff on the field right in front of me that I'll never see again. My third favourite, because he looked like a geek, but when he crossed that white line and took off those glasses he became superman, was John Worsfold. What Woosha did in that first derby was great as he basically went up to Winston Abraham and said,

"Go near the ball, Winston, and I'm going to break you." Winston never got a kick.'

The derby is an important game for Stasiuk and the coming of the Dockers into the AFL is something he has a certain view on, which relates to the perceived dominance of the West and the powers in the East wanting to curb it. 'They don't want dynasties outside of Victoria. The Dockers were brought in for two reasons and two reasons only: to dilute the power of the Eagles and to make the Victorians happy. So they get the Dockers in, hoping we will die, but look at 2006 – we lost both derbies but we won the grand final.'

Stasiuk leans forward as much for emphasis as to deliver a message, pointing out that the derby has its seeds planted in the old WAFL allegiances. Despite being so staunch in these allegiances, and conveying to us how important football has been to him since he was a boy, he has something he wants to get off his chest. 'Let's get this straight: it is a derby first and foremost, it's not a *darby* – that's a horse race. The derby to me is old-school. I grew up with East Perth. I can't stand West Perth. I know East Fremantle and South Fremantle supporters hate one another. The Dockers and Eagles is an extension of that. I know the media love the rivalry but I also think the media have got to get off this line of every time it's the derby then *it's the biggest derby ever*. The biggest derby hasn't happened yet. That will be a grand final. I think statistically the effects are glaring, in that there's more losses after a derby for both sides. My brother Shane pointed it out the other day. He said, "I don't want to see a derby final unless it's a grand final because it won't benefit either side. If it's an elimination final it won't do any team any good."'

Stasiuk sits back and scratches his head and pauses for a moment, reflecting on what a derby grand final would mean to him personally. 'I don't know if I could handle it, because I can't watch derbies at the moment. Derbies are strange things and they do strange things to people. I used to have people come over my house back in the day but my old man wanted to fight my Dockers mates. I was starting to get hives with the derby hype, and it's stupid thinking of how it affected me. Imagine the players and what they have to go through.'

Just how crazy things could become occurred after one particular derby that resulted in a Freo victory. 'I can't remember exactly what game it was, but I remember I went with my mate, my brother and my Uncle Bill Hayward, who is a big Dockers man. The Dockers won, and afterwards outside the oval I could hear the beeping of a car horn, and I could see this car weaving through traffic going quite fast. It stopped right in front of the Subiaco Hotel on Hay Street. The driver had the big purple flag hanging out the car and I was pissed off so I grabbed the flag as they went past. I threw it on the ground and they slammed their brakes on and they got out the car. I said, "Do you want your flag?" I picked up the flag and snapped it in half. I yelled, "This is Subiaco and Eagles territory – why don't you fuck off back to Freo!" We all went into the Subiaco Hotel and had a few beers. We then headed back out and there were cops, Dockers and Eagles supporters punching into each other. It was like the Wild West. I started the fire. I thought I was flying the flag or, in this case literally cracking the flag, and almost started a riot. It wasn't great behaviour, I'm not proud of it.'

It is the place that Stasiuk's passion for West Coast comes from, that an equally passionate dislike also springs for some Dockers players. 'I couldn't stand watching The Wiz [Jeff Farmer] run around. Look, he was good, he's my blood for Christ's sake, but jeez he was antagonistic. If I saw Ballantyne in the street I would probably say something to him. I don't like him because he's a prick. I would love to have Worsfold walking up to Ballantyne and saying, "You go near that ball, I'm going to break your neck." In saying that, Mundy's a gun and very underrated. Fyfe's great but he's a flash player. Mundy, he'd be in my side any day of the week.'

Despite the intensity of his feelings for his side, it is clear that in some respects Glen's perception of football has changed over the years. So much so, that he has changed his mind when it comes to Fremantle being the easybeats of the competition. He has also had time to reconsider what his passion actually means – no less potent perhaps, but not as amplified as it once was. '[Fremantle] will win one [a grand final] eventually, it won't be nice from my point of view, but life will go on. For me, I have settled down now and I don't take the footy so seriously. That's because I've got two kids to bring up. They know I'm passionate about my football, but in the end, you know, it's *football*. It's great, but it's football, and at the end of the day we've all got to get along in this town called Perth. But, saying that, one of my girls switched allegiances to the Sydney Swans last year (because of Buddy of course) and though I wasn't happy with her decision I said to them as long as it isn't the bloody Dockers – I just might disown you if you did.'

BEVAN TAYLOR – EAGLES

For many people, Lake Grace is a town they might have heard of in passing without knowing exactly where it is, but that all changed in late September 2015. Situated in the south-east of Western Australia, Lake Grace is one of the largest agricultural shires in the state, known mainly for being a sheep- and wheat-growing area. When Nat Fyfe, the Fremantle Dockers champion midfielder and Lake Grace local, won the most coveted individual award in football, the Brownlow Medal, the telecast from Melbourne made a live cross to the Lake Grace Hotel, which was packed to the rafters with locals celebrating the hometown boy's big win. Somewhere in that crowd was Bevan Taylor, Eagles member, sheep cocky, Nicky Winmar's landlord and former champion junior athlete for Aquinas. In the days after the Fyfe win, the locals mobilised to commemorate this once-in-a-lifetime event. For Bevan, who also runs a canvassing business on top of his farming, the task was to create a massive thirty-five metre banner that read *Welcome to Nat Fyfe Country: Home of the 2015 Brownlow Medal Winner*. For a hardcore Eagles man, the irony was not lost on him as he searched the internet for shots of Fyfe to place on the big sign.

This was not the first time Bevan had been struck by the irony of following the Eagles but being razzed up by irritating Dockers paraphernalia. In 2012 he had bought numerous tickets in the Lake Grace footy club raffle. First prize was a signed Dockers jumper that Fyfe himself had organised and sent down. What Bevan really wanted though was second prize, a trailer-load of mallee roots. As the night rolled on and the beer and party pies flowed, fate stepped in. First prize in the raffle was drawn. Taylor won the signed Dockers jumper. He took it all in good humour but also half-jested, 'I now *really* wanted that load of mallee roots so I could go home, start a big bloody fire and throw that awful looking Dockers guernsey right on top.' Bevan did not win the firewood and instead he had the jumper framed. It's now in his shed, where he watches footy and goes to unwind.

For Bevan, sport in country Australia is vitally important. 'In a small country community, it all comes back to sport. Some people who are not into sport would probably disagree, but really if you want to get to know people and get involved in a country town, it's the football club, netball club, tennis club, bowls that makes such a strong bind. I haven't been involved in the footy club for a number of years but even now the guys know who you are.' Taylor continues, 'Football was my biggest love, but I played tennis and I did athletics at a state level as a middle-distance runner when I was a teen.' Bevan drains his cup of tea and smiles at the memories that football has provided him, playing in what was a very skilled country league. 'Mark Bairstow came back from Geelong that one year he played for Lake Grace and we made the elimination final. We went through to play in the grandee and got belted by Boddington. But there has been a lot of great footballers come out of here. Our Shire President, Andy Walker, when asked about footy talent in the district after Nat won the Brownlow, said we can fill a London bus with AFL players if you drew a hundred-kilometre circle around Lake Grace.'

For Bevan, his allegiance with the West Coast Eagles was something that was piqued early and grew with early success. 'They were our WA side and were playing off in a grand final within four years. We got sledged a bit with people from across Australia saying that it was a state team but the bulk of that first team I reckon was just about all Fremantle. Ironically, when the Dockers joined in 1995 it was just about all past and current Claremont players. And to think we get called the "chardonnay set". My sister says that all the time, and it drives me mental.' Taylor stays with the theme of his family, many of whom are Dockers supporters, labelling his father, Peter 'Spud' Taylor, a turncoat. 'Dad was an Eagles supporter for a long time and then he became a Dockers member.' Bevan shakes his head and continues, 'I never even considered it. I even went to Aquinas with the inaugural Dockers captain Benji Allan, played with him too. The thought never crossed my mind.' Bevan goes on to qualify perhaps the reason he did not change teams has something to do with the success of the Eagles early on, compared to the Dockers' dismal early years. 'The Dockers used to have this habit of recruiting really good footballers and turning them into shit. Des Headland was a classic example, an absolute world-beater up at Brisbane, then at the Dockers he battled to get a kick. Belly would have been the only exception but they let him go, got him back and paid a motza.'

Bevan laughs at the absurdity of the Dockers' early history and their battling ways. He then cites some champions from the Eagles who set themselves apart from the Dockers. 'I still reckon Ben Cousins is the best footballer that has ever gone through the Eagles. Just his work ethic. It's a real shame what ended up happening, and people keep saying that the 2006 flag was tainted, and that shits me. Adam Hunter was probably also one of my favourite Eagles. But then if you go right back to the early days, I would say Mark Zanotti stood out.' Bevan recalls seeing the very first western derby which came at a crucial time of the farming calendar: seeding. 'I reckon the first western derby the old man had us on the tractor and there was no way that I was going to sit on that tractor while the western derby was on and I said, "We'll shut down." I went home and watched the footy. Felt bloody great jumping back in, singing the Eagles song.'

Bevan looks forward to derby games because of what it means in his community. 'I think what the derby comes down to is bragging rights. I think they are the closest things to a finals game we have, and if the Dockers win, that spoils my whole weekend. That's how much it affects me.' He lets out a rolling laugh. 'For so long the Dockers had this mentality that it is all about beating the West Coast Eagles. I just couldn't get it. Then they play like shit the following week and sometimes the rest of the year. But come derby time they would try to punch the crap out of the Eagles and it was just about one or two games a year. There were other teams out there, and it stuck out like dogs' balls, I reckon.'

Bevan's favourite derby moment featured Dockers small forward Hayden Ballantyne. 'When Ballantyne hit the post and they could have won it, but instead they lost by a point, it was great. If anyone else had kicked that point you'd feel a bit sorry. He shits me to tears but if he was on your side you'd love him to bits.'

Bevan believes that there will be a derby grand final. 'There will be one for sure. But they need Fyfe to stay when he becomes a free agent. He needs to do a Pav and stay with the Dockers.' Where will he watch the game? 'I really love watching the footy on telly. We've got a shed at home with a projector and a big screen, a hammock and a beer fridge. That's if Nicky Winmar can't get me a ticket.' It might seem like Bevan is name-dropping, but the encounter with one of the game's greats came about by chance. 'I got a phone call from this woman, asking me if I had a house on the farm for rent. I said you can come out and have a look. They get out of the car and it is Nicky Winmar. He stuck out his hand said, "I'm Nicky," and I said, "Yeah I know."' Bevan laughs at the memory, pleased that Winmar was able to get a ticket for his son Tom to attend the 2015 grand final.

But if there ever is a derby grand final, and the Eagles win, Bevan looks forward to Nat Fyfe driving the family truck out to the Taylor farm. 'Nat came back to drive a truck at harvest time for a few days recently and I did ask him how he was going and whatnot. We had a chat, and I tried to make myself a little bit taller, a little bit bulkier, as I was standing next to him.' Bevan probably won't say much about the grand final because after all what could be said? Nat Fyfe, like Bevan Taylor, is still a Lake Grace boy at heart.

ALSY MACDONALD – DOCKERS

Alsy Macdonald is currently the Senior Legal Officer at the Equal Opportunity Commission in Western Australia, but he's better known as one of the founding members of the seminal Western Australian rock band The Triffids, the first Australian band to appear on the cover of UK rock street-bible *NME*. With enthralling stories of life on the road in the UK and Europe, and his expansive knowledge on topics ranging from politics, cars, science and obscure 1960s advertising jingles, Macdonald's key ability is not just his knowledge of the big topics but also his capacity to tell a story. He also has a keen appreciation of small, everyday things. One Tuesday night, when meeting up with two other Dockers desperadoes for a regular Tuesday night guerrilla podcast, *The Purple Circus*, Macdonald pulled out his newest East Fremantle membership trinket: a beautiful faux-'50s bottle-opener with a blue and white enamel finish. Everybody in the 'studio' agreed that the opener was indeed a thing of beauty as Alsy insisted on opening every stubbie that night, despite them being twist tops.

Settling in on a crisp afternoon in his East Fremantle home, it becomes clear from the get-go that, for Alsy and his family (his wife is The Triffids keyboardist Jill Birt), football is not just a passing interest but central to daily life. 'I grew up in a household that already had football very much on the agenda. I played juniors for Dalkeith Nedlands for three years and then I was in the Hollywood High School football team, one that was similar to *The Bad News Bears*. I played on a wing. I wore an oversized, scratchy old woollen jumper and dunder-clumping footy boots that made you look like a clown when you ran.' Macdonald rumbles with laughter at the memory. 'Playing for Hollywood High, I recall a footy carnival on a shocking day in year ten. Stephen Malaxos was our captain, and I remember kicking the ball and the wind taking it out of bounds. That was my one possession for the game. Malaxos kicked seven goals and single-handedly won the game off his own boot.' Even if he was not that great on the paddock, Alsy did go to many WAFL games and as a young boy followed Claremont. 'At around five or six years of age, I became conscious that my dad would take my older brothers to Claremont Oval to watch the Tiges play. My dad and brothers were into it, despite Claremont getting regular shellackings. But as I got older and by, say, age twelve or thirteen, I had the bug.'

The winter months were taken up with a regular diet of local football, the VFL and rock'n'roll. These worlds would collide especially on Sunday night. 'The WAFL back then wasn't diluted by a national comp. Saturday was spent at Tigerland and Sunday it was a one-two combination of *Countdown* and *The Winners*. It's hard to explain to our kids what Sunday was like. Dad would drift in just before six pm as he was getting ready for the start of *The Winners*, raise his eyebrows and walk out until he heard the opening strains of *The Winners* theme song fresh from Abba's "Fernando" for the umpteenth time.'

Alsy vividly recalls the 1972 WAFL grand final between his beloved Tigers and East Perth, where he listened at home to the game on the wireless. 'It was a wet, cold day and there were fifty thousand people crammed into Subi Oval on the terraces, and the Bright Spot Burger van was working overtime. That was my first football heartbreak – the Claremont '72 loss, but it instilled something in me. It's hard to explain, but people who create music or literature or something else, are constantly trying to get to something that is better than what they've done before; hope is an incredible driver. And I think football from then on encapsulated a mystery that was bound up in hope. I understood it a bit better with that loss.'

When The Triffids had essentially finished up in 1990, both Alsy and Jill Birt returned to Australia. Alsy found himself wondering who these Eagles *were*, as they were causing a great deal of unrest to sides in the East. This became quite evident when in 1991 Mick Malthouse took the Eagles to their first grand final that was held at Waverley where they lost to Hawthorn by fifty-three points. 'It was a really quick escalation by West Coast. The Waverley game was famous because the G was being renovated and it was the game Angry Anderson tore it up in the Batmobile. Who can forget? In 1992 West Coast won the grand final but I was never attracted to the Eagles and by '94 I wanted the Cats to win, which they didn't, tragically. But it was also the year before the creation of Freo and they were being talked about. I thought, "Isn't this great? At least now there'll be a team that is associated with a locality, and that gives due acknowledgement and credibility to the Fremantle football legacy." I thought, "I want to be a fan of this team at the ground floor." It was great to be there at the beginning in the Neesham years. It was a huge experiment, that sometimes worked and sometimes didn't. I think we knew within two or three years that this was going to be a bit of a roller-coaster ride. No romantic trajectory like West Coast.'

That lack of romance was made all too clear when Alsy's two sons came home from school one day and shared a nursery rhyme with their father that was floating around the playground. 'Connor was eight that year and Oscar was six, and they were going to East Fremantle Primary School.

They had friends who went for the Eagles and there was a nursery rhyme that went "Freo, way to go / lost nine derbies in row / West Coast going to give them the old heave ho / We are the Freo shockers"'. It was from this that Alsy's favourite derby moment emerged, as the Dockers looked set to lose ten derbies in a row. 'Connor was coming along to games and we noticed that all the games he came to, we won. In the end I was sort of press-ganging Connor to come. Things unfolded in a very strange way that day; even the weather was doing funny things. It had been drizzling a little bit, and it was an Eagles home game. In front of some thirty-seven thousand Eagles fans, Freo started coming back. There was electricity in the air and it started drizzling harder in the last quarter. Tony Modra kicked that amazing goal. Then the siren went and there was a very light misty haze over the ground then a double rainbow came out at the city end, because the sun shone through. How's that for symbolism? It was almost like a glimpse of a possible future. After losing the first nine derbies, we have nearly squared the ledger, and I still have the ticket from that first win.'

For Alsy, those early years of struggle also define his feelings towards particular favourite players. He compares this with the Eagles. 'West Coast had some truly standout brilliant players over the journey. Freo had to kind of wait for its genius players. Getting the Wizard and Tony Modra springs to mind. I think the Pav story is such a great story and you just had a sense he was going to stick around for a long while. Jill and I first started taking the kids to see Freo play then – they grew up with Pav.'

It was also during this formative period that Alsy came to understand what the derby rivalry means to him. 'You've got to be honest, and say the derby does mean something, and I know that, in professional football-speak, teams will downplay it. They'll say it's just another game, et cetera, et cetera, but we know that's a load of bullshit. The derby means something, and it certainly means something to the fans. It probably doesn't mean as much to Freo fans as it once did because the ledger's been squared so convincingly.'

The Macdonald family have no particular rituals around the derby games, except logistical ones. In saying that, Alsy's sons have taken to gently mocking him when the Dockers lose. 'My sons tease me when we get back to the car. Oscar says, "Don't give me one of your philosophical *it's not the end of the world* pep talks, okay." I have been known to do that, but you have got to give them something to hope for. Although I don't want a derby grand final. I tend to be a bit more grounded in my dreams and aspirations but that is a bridge too far. To pit those teams against each other in the grand final – the stakes are too high. To win would be almost unimaginable, but to lose – I wonder whether the loser would ever really recover? The loser may never get the chance for revenge. I think back to the Eagles' really successful era when just about every West Coast player in those games was a vaudeville act: a guy in a top hat with a cape and an oily moustache and that chunderous jumper that they wore, that's what it would be like again. Even if Freo came back the next year, and beat some other team in the grand final, the loss in a grand final to the mob up the road doesn't bear thinking about.'

For the time being, a Fremantle grand final win is the stuff of fantasy although, like all Dockers fans, Alsy dares to dream. 'The message to the Freo folk is hang in there. When we finally win the premiership it will be far more special than any West Coast fan could ever know. Let's hope we don't have to wait too long.'

DEANNE LEWIS – DOCKERS

The name Lewis is one that is inextricably linked to the early story of the West Coast Eagles. A perennial crowd favourite, Chris Lewis was a footballer who was greatly admired. An Eagles Club Champion in 1990, he was also a member of their 1992 and 1994 premiership sides. Chris is Deanne's cousin. With a career that commenced in 1987, the same year the Eagles did, Lewis finished up in 2000 having played 215 games and kicking 259 goals. His distinguished career was capped off with him being named in the forward pocket of the AFL's Indigenous Team of the Century in 2005. It is therefore intriguing to meet his cousin Deanne, who is a Dockers supporter. Deanne gained her degree in Indigenous Community Health at Curtin University some twenty years ago, and has been employed as the Aboriginal Hospital Liaison Coordinator with North Metropolitan Health Service for the last twelve months. We agree to meet at the South Fremantle clubrooms to hear her journey.

'Having a cousin that played in the AFL back in the '80s was interesting. As a teenager in high school you'd go up to the shops and meet Chris. We'd be sitting on one side of those big planter boxes and Chris and I are having a yarn and catching up and you could hear people behind whispering, "That's Chris Lewis, that's Chris Lewis." I'd be like, *damn*, he's a normal person, he's my cousin and we're just trying to have a catch up. Most people that met me in those years, especially the girls, would say, "Can you tell Chris that I love him?" I'd just raise my eyebrows and say, "Get to the back of the line," because it happened all the time.'

Despite the adulation for Chris, it wasn't easy going to games and watching her cousin getting knocked around, and she was mindful of the toll that being a professional footballer had on family commitments. 'Watching a family member on an AFL field really gets your heart going, and it was hard seeing him get hit. I'd be sitting at Subiaco Oval closing my eyes to all that stuff. Then there were the times you would be hearing people call his name, like "Lewey, Lewey". It just gives you goosebumps. It's amazing. But despite all of that, it was hard for Christopher because he missed out on a lot of family events and made a lot of sacrifices for his football. When you've got a family member out there it's really emotional. Lots of ups and downs, like with that biting incident with Todd Viney. The whole family was very low-profile about it, but even Auntie [Lorna Lewis, Chris Lewis's mum] had all this media outside the house. It was explained to me by saying that "if I stuck my hand down your throat what would be your first reaction?" The bite wasn't intentional, but that's how it was interpreted by the media.'

Deanne's first football love was with the Claremont Football Club, where Chris's father, her Uncle Irwin, was a premiership player. 'I'm a Tigers girl all the way. My Uncle Irwin played in the 1964 grand final. And all of his sons played for Claremont. Then there is the Yamatji connection with Michael Mitchell. Mitch's auntie married my uncle so, we are all the same mob from the same area.' The other connection was where all the families lived in Perth, and the connectivity sport had with their extended family networks. 'Nan lived in Karrinyup and lived on the corner of Ramsay and Dean Street, and there was a park across the road. The Headlands lived up the road, the Taylors and the Martins were also around the corner. We'd all head over and play cricket. You had to catch the ball, you could not drop catches, you had to throw the ball properly or you'd get drilled by your brothers and cousins. It was full-on.'

It's clear that sport played a big part in the extended Lewis family life, and the centrepiece of this was football and the diehard allegiance with the West Coast Eagles. So the question that needs to be asked is: how did Deanne Lewis become a Docker, and live to tell the tale? Deanne throws her head back and laughs. 'With my background and being an Eagles member, I was fortunately pressured by my partner Rod Ryder, and instead of us being in-laws we became *outlaws*. This wasn't long after Christopher's retirement – maybe two or three years – and Rod kept nagging and nagging for me to become a Docker as he always had his heart in Fremantle, but I flat-out refused. He did not let up. Then one day we went to a derby and he kept at it. I was stupid enough to say, "Whoever wins this game we'll be the members of next year." The bloody Dockers won! This was a time when Freo were winyarn [hopeless] and not winning very many games. Not in my wildest dreams did I think they were going to win. When I told my family they were like "Noooo!!!" But I just thought Christopher's not playing anymore, and there were a lot of blackfellas at Freo and they seemed pretty supportive of Aboriginal people. I think at the time they probably had the highest number of Aboriginal players. So I said, "What the hell."'

Deanne smiles as she reflects upon the fallout from such a dramatic course of action. 'I've been blacklisted big-time. You can't be a Lewis and be a Dockers member. When I used to go to Auntie's, they'd always take the piss out of me. I'd dress up a grandchild in Dockers gear and appeal to my auntie's soft side. She was always soft on the grannies when they were babies. Also, my mum was always Chris's favourite auntie, so that helped. Then on Facebook I'd cop a lot of shit from cousins. During the season one in particular does not shut up running down the Dockers. I said to him once, "I actually think you're a closet Dockers fan because you talk more about them than you do West Coast."'

Does Deanne ever regret her decision to stay true to her bet with her partner on that fateful day? 'Nup. I mean, West Coast are okay but they're also a bunch of arseholes. I've made the move and I've copped all the backlash and quite frankly I don't care, Freo are my team now and that's it. And I just think Freo is great in their support of Aboriginal players. They're a great community club. Over time and in the work that I do to help promote health in the Aboriginal community, we've had Jeff Farmer, Dessie Headland, Michael Johnson and Antoni Grover doing their certificates in alcohol and drugs. I also thought Dion Woods and Roger Hayden were wonderful footballers. Roger was a very fair player, and he and Dion always seemed to have a lot of time on the field.'

Despite this, for Deanne the hardest thing about losing a derby is the fallout from the game. 'It is crap. You cop it. But lately it's been nice to have it over the so-called "big brother" at home. It just kind of puts them back in their place a little bit. They can get a bit feral, but I suppose they are the first side from West Australia to come into the VFL and in a sense they're very protective of it. And we've beaten them enough now. They're not worth gloating over anymore. Now it's about beating Sydney and Hawthorn and bringing them down.'

Before we let Deanne get back to work, we ask her whether she ever wagers anything on the derby games. She smiles before replying, 'Nope, I do not bet on derbies, no way. I'm still getting over the last bet!'

JESSE DART – DOCKERS

Plucked from obscurity, six-year-old Jesse Dart shot to national fame on *The Footy Show* in 2007. As football identity Sam Newman scoured the malls and shopping precincts of Fremantle town, it was Jesse's father Graeme who noticed the Geelong champion looking for subjects for the show's frequently maligned 'Street Talk' segment. With a little encouragement from his dad, little Jesse moved into Newman's orbit and the roving eye of the camera. Due to his beguiling innocence and candid perspectives on his beloved Dockers, Jesse was propelled immediately into hundreds of thousands of homes across Australia, and for the next few years he rode the media wave, making him something of an unofficial figurehead for the club.

Sitting up in the East Fremantle grandstand, I ask Jesse what it was like to be a TV star at such a young age. He giggles and recounts how it happened. 'Me and my dad had just been to Fremantle to the movies to see one of the *Shrek* films. I was six at the time. We're walking through Kings Square right where Dymocks used to be and Dad said, "Look, Jesse, there's Sam Newman." I didn't know who he was because I hadn't watched *The Footy Show* before because it was way past my bedtime, which was eight-thirty pm. So Dad wandered over towards Sam, and Sam was thinking Dad wanted to talk to him. Dad's like, "Talk to him," pointing at me. I don't remember much of being spoken to, only what you can see on YouTube. Then maybe a week or two later I was invited over to Melbourne and actually went on the show. They put an old '90s-style Dockers jumper on me and I talked away. Then they got me back again for the grand final show. I remember looking out at the crowd and thinking, "Wow."'

Such was the impact of Jesse's appearance that he became something of a Western Australian celebrity, leading to further media opportunities. 'I had a bit of a thing with 92.9 FM for a while and I also got called back a few times for Channel Seven's and Nine's finals coverage, and stuff like that. It was really cool.'

Yet despite his instant exposure, Jesse did experience some negativity from being a Dockers supporter in the limelight. 'I remember in one of the games I attended as the Dockers number-one junior ticket holder, I was sworn at by one of the West Coast fans and that kind of put me off them altogether. I don't know what actually happened but I was probably just saying something to Ben Cousins like, "You're a waste of space, Cousins," and the Eagles fan then swore at me. But having that gig was great. I got to meet a lot of the players down at training. One of my favourite footy memories was when Mark Harvey gave me a whistle and told me to do whatever I wanted, so I made Pavlich hurry up and finish his lap.'

Jesse shakes his head at the memories. He then gives a very detailed account as to how his dual football interests in East Fremantle and the Dockers took shape. 'I know it sounds very clichéd but I really love football. I love the Sharks [East Fremantle] and that is saying something, because the first game I remember was a one hundred and fifty point loss to South Fremantle. I would say my love of the Sharks is on par with my love for the Dockers. Like the ground here, it's not the prettiest but it's got that history. Such as the Dockers playing their first sanctioned match here against Essendon in 1995.'

Jesse describes the role his parents played in developing his love for the game. 'My mum's been the main figure in my life, and she's a Carlton supporter. But I guess Dad was my main influence in terms of football. He got me to play Auskick and got me my first footy cards, which really helped me to remember the players. My dad's always been a Dockers supporter ever since they came into the competition, so I don't think that I was ever going to be a Blues man.' Like his love for both the Dockers and East Fremantle, Jesse's footy heroes are obscure choices but he sticks by them no matter what. 'I always loved Pavlich but I've always gone for guys that have to work week in and week out to keep their spot. For me Scotty Thornton was that guy. Rhys Palmer too. Thornton was the guy I ran out with through the banner in 2008 against Collingwood.'

Jesse also has very clear aspirations for what he wants to do after completing school, which is being a football commentator. 'If my mates and I are just kicking the ball around I just find myself commentating, it's like a natural thing. It's strange but it's something I love doing. For me, Basil Zempilas is annoying. How did he ever get a television job commentating? I was better at seven years old than Zempilas will ever be.'

Jesse is equally scathing of the seemingly fickle nature of West Coast supporters when they are at games. 'I think West Coast fans generally are a bit more edgy when it comes to watching their football. I mean, a lot of the times I see West Coast fans leaving games early if they are losing and to me that's something no fan should ever do.' For Jesse the derby is a very specific Western Australian phenomenon that has transcended the game and other sporting rivalries across Australia. 'A derby is more than just rivalry. I mean, there's Carlton and Collingwood, and there's Port Adelaide and Adelaide, but for me the derby is two established heavyweights of the competition going hard at it. Like compare it to Brisbane and Gold Coast. It's the most boring rivalry I've ever seen. They barely get ten people to a game. And what does the QClash actually mean? It is a terrible name for anything. The Battle of the Bridge in Sydney is even worse – it just doesn't make any sense. I mean, Port Adelaide and Adelaide fans, sure they are passionate, but it's just nowhere as loud as as it is at Subiaco Oval.' Jesse cites his most memorable derby moments to make the point. 'The derby moments I remember the most are the ones that hurt the most. I can remember like it was yesterday Ballantyne celebrating like he won the game and then watching the ball hit the post. I also loved Shauny Mac's last game, and the fact that Shauny Mac had been such a great servant to the club and he was bowing out and we were going out to win for him. I find that West Coast supporters – if they win they will talk about it for weeks. Then they come out with stupid slogans like *The West is Ours*.' Despite the irritation that the 'mob up the road' seem to instil in Jesse, he makes light of the situation. 'I've had a bit of fun with my teachers now and then. If I get any West Coast teachers and it's a derby I will bet them to be a Docker for a day. Luckily I have never had to wear those awful colours because every time the wager is on we've always won.'

KIA MIPPY – EAGLES

Kia Mippy is a Yamatji woman whose family originates from Carnarvon. Kia has worked in the tertiary education sector for several years mainly at the Centre for Aboriginal Studies at Curtin University. In her time at Curtin she has had several roles, from student support, receptionist, personal assistant and now as a financial officer in human resources. Kia understands the value of hard work, as her father worked in construction, drilling holes for power poles for the causeway between Karratha and Dampier, before moving to Victoria. It was here that Kia was born, and where she learned what being staunch is all about. It's easy to laugh about it now, when she is back in Western Australia and the West Coast heartland, but as a young girl growing up in Geelong, Kia regularly felt the wrath of Cats supporters. This had everything to do with her unwavering allegiance to the West Coast Eagles, a side that the Cats lost to in both the 1992 and 1994 AFL grand finals. This made going to school in Geelong hard for Kia and going to Kardinia Park, on rare occasions, with her family to watch West Coast. These were 'not nice at all. They all hated West Coast, and I was the brunt of a lot of people's anger. I remember there were a couple of crazy football matches at Kardinia Park when the Eagles came to Geelong. I was fourteen and we were leaving the ground and I got scruffed up by a forty-year-old man because West Coast beat the Cats. He grabbed me by my scarf and like, *pulled it*. It scared the hell out of me. But it's funny that when I left Geelong when I was twenty-one and returned to WA I was really excited, thinking everyone's going to go for West Coast, but interestingly most people I know seem to go for Freo.'

Football has always been part of Kia's life and a positive influence in many ways. 'As my Dad is from Carnarvon he followed the WAFL and he has always been a West Perth man. But before West Coast he went for North Melbourne. As soon as there was a West Australian team, he jumped, and the Eagles were his team. So since I was born it's been West Coast for me. I was born West Coast. He didn't have to force it on me because that is what I grew up with. It was normal. Footy was always just there, like part of the family.'

Despite her allegiance during the season Kia watches as much football as she can on television and keeps up to date with what is going on with the AFL online and in the newspapers. 'I just love it. I don't know why, I just do. I can literally sit and watch more than half of the games on the weekends. I love how they play, I love the players, I love some teams, I hate some teams. But the game itself I love. The marks, the goals. It's insane, there's nothing like it. I like the way the Hawks play and North Melbourne, because that's my dad's old team. Eddie Betts and Cyril Rioli are favourite players, as is Jack Zeibell because he goes in hard.'

Which brings us to her favourite West Coast player – the man who encapsulated what West Coast stands for. 'Ben Cousins was my favourite, I loved him because he just chopped up on the field, it was always number nine for me. I also loved Beau Waters. He was the enforcer at West Coast. We didn't have much of that type of player in our team. Josh Kennedy is also awesome – he can mark it and kick it and he's big and imposing.'

For Kia, the derbies have provided her with a very specific view of what the Dockers represent. 'There was not any instant hate of them. Not to start with anyway. But when

I watched the Demolition Derby with all the fights, I was like, "I don't really like this much." So now when the derby is played, I don't like playing Fremantle. To me they're the crappy little brother to the best team in the West. That's what my brother and I say about Freo: they are the crappy little brother. And the derby is a chance for us to pound those guys into the ground. I don't treat it as a grand final or anything, but they are probably the most intense games of the season, it's bruising. I think the players and the teams themselves play differently. It's definitely more aggressive than usual. I don't mean what happened a couple of years back with Dale Kickett punching on with everyone, it is just more brutal than a usual game.'

Kia prepares herself differently for derbies than she does for other games, due to what the derby means to her. 'I'm going to sound crazy but I get butterflies. I always make sure I paint my fingernails West Coast colours. I can't sit still so I walk around the house and I pace a lot. I'm usually okay until it starts, and then I'm on edge all the time. It just freaks me out. I always wear my jacket and my scarf from Tuesday until Sunday as I think it might bring West Coast more luck, particularly at work when there is purple crap everywhere. If we lose then I usually get over it. But it depends, because if people rub it in, that's when I get upset and angry. It rankles me, because I don't do that if West Coast win. I don't rub it in to Freo people because that's bad karma and you get it back.'

Perhaps it is this karmic logic that saw Kia enjoy one of her most memorable derby wins in 2011. 'Ballantyne hitting the post was great, because Freo were going to win and then they didn't. We were at the pub in Success called *The Gate*. It went right off. I had a bet with a Fremantle supporter who was giving me hell all night about it. It was only a free drink, but it made me feel good. The pub was just all Freo, there was only me, my brother and a couple of others that were West Coast and everyone else was Freo. The pub cleared out pretty quick after the game. It was awesome.'

Kia is ambivalent about the potential for a derby grand final. 'I'd lose my mind. I don't know if it would be good to have really. I would not want Freo to win because they would not be that crappy little brother anymore. The Victorians would not be very happy either, but if there was a grand final and the Eagles won, then that would be sensational.' So who would Kia choose to take the final kick with the West Coasters five points down just as the final siren goes? She does not miss a beat. 'LeCras. If anyone had to kick for my life I would most definitely choose Mark LeCras.'

GLENIS FREEMANTLE – DOCKERS

It is hard to find good staff these days. Just ask Glenis Freemantle (yes, that is her surname), supervisor of The Vege Patch cafe located right next to the Tim Winton Lecture Theatre at Curtin University. Glenis is a quietly staunch member of the Dockers. She has travelled all over Australia, even to the frozen wasteland of Tasmania's Aurora Stadium, to watch her beloved team play. Sadly, on all of these outings, she has never witnessed an interstate win. Despite this, her heart is as purple as the blood that flows in her veins. So you can imagine the look of complete surprise when one day Fremantle midfielder and Dockers favourite Michael Barlow walked into The Vege Patch and placed his order for a flat white and a salami baguette, toasted no less. Glenis pushed her colleague, Gordon the West Coast Eagles–supporting barista aside, and made what she called 'the most perfectly delivered coffee in history.' She gave strict instructions to the counter staff to make sure the baguette also arrived in the same way. Glenis went into her small office to compose herself. She texted a few girlfriends with the news and then five minutes later popped her head out and noticed Micky B still hovering around. He looked uncomfortable and hungry. More minutes ticked past and Glenis became increasingly aware of Barlow's agitation, imagining she could hear his tummy rumbling from over the sound of Gordon's preferred station, 6IX. 'I couldn't understand why he was hanging around for so long. One of the staff was clueless as to who he was. There was also a communication breakdown between the person who took the order and the one I told to keep an eye on it [the salami baguette]. Consequently it burnt and needed redoing. It was soooo embarrassing, but Michael was very nice about it, of course. As a consequence of this, all of my staff have been educated on the identity of Dockers players since then.'

For Glenis, it is her surname that gives away her allegiance to the Dockers. In saying this, Glenis wants to make one thing absolutely clear about how she came to get it. 'It's Freemantle spelt with a double "e". But I don't barrack for the Fremantle Dockers *because* of my name, contrary to popular belief. That's what everybody thinks and it annoys me. They say, "Oh, you must barrack for the Dockers?" Yeah, I do, but that's not why. I married in 1990 and I didn't know there was going to be a Fremantle Dockers so when I heard that there was a Fremantle team coming, I thought, "This is going to be my team, it's just perfect." But I didn't source my husband out just for his name, contrary to other people's beliefs. I was ready for them when they came into the competition.'

Glenis's journey through football is a personal one and one that has deep connections to her father. It even meant that for a brief time that she was connected to the West Coast Eagles, although she insists that she has had several long showers because of that history and that she no longer has any feelings for them at all. 'The reason I barrack for the Dockers is because my father had four daughters and he was a big East Fremantle man. My sisters and I loved it, and I can remember a few grand finals there at the clubrooms, such great memories.' So big a name in fact was Glenis's father that Ron Alexander, the Eagle's inaugural coach, got Jim Hurst a job in an official capacity. 'In 1987 when the Eagles came along, I was like twenty or twenty-one. Ron Alexander was made coach, and my dad was working at East Fremantle as the team manager for Old Easts. So Ron took Dad with him and my dad was team manager for the Eagles in their first year, so I barracked for the Eagles. Dad used to be able to get us into the clubrooms and I got some photos with Eagles like Adrian Barich, David Hart and Michael O'Connell, who I kind of swooned over in those days. But then unfortunately Ron got sacked, and my dad got sacked too.'

After the sacking of her father, and due to his Fremantle football heritage, Glenis's interest in the Dockers was aroused, slowly but surely. 'I was going to barrack for them right from the start, but I didn't become a member because I had little kids. Actually, my second son was born in '95 so I just started going to games when they got a bit older. I became a member after the year they were in their first final against Essendon. I used to buy tickets randomly, and I remember queuing up to get two tickets to the final at Ticketmaster at Carousel. I just got to the counter and they said, "Sold out." I went back to work and I said, right, I'm going to become a member. So I became a member and it's been so good. There's a dad that sits in front of me and he's been going with his three daughters. We got our membership the same year. My husband's a Richmond supporter so he doesn't come along. So these little kids sitting in front of me are now eighteen- and nineteen-year-olds. It's just great.'

Glenis's love of the code also means the time and space to relax. 'For me it's purely entertainment. I love Freo and I would rather watch a football game on TV of two teams that I don't care about than do a lot of other things. It's an outing for me, it's somewhere I go every second week with my kids. It's a release, it gets your mind off other things and it's sharing time with people that care about the same thing you care about.'

It's from the position of her membership seats that Glenis has had the thrill of watching some of Fremantle's greats ply their trade. 'I don't know why, but I loved Shaun McManus. He was real. I don't know whether it was true but I remember hearing him say that he could have nominated for the draft the year before the Dockers came out, but he held back to wait because he knew the team was coming. I think that's the definition of loyalty. He wasn't all that flashy but he tried so hard. I liked Chris Mayne; maybe it's the curls. I liked Paul Haselby too. He just seemed like a real larrikin. I like Peter Bell, Luke McPharlin and Jessie Sinclair was cute-as. And I liked Michael Barlow because he comes into our shop. But seriously, he is very reliable. I don't dislike anyone. I hear people around me criticising players like Zac Dawson. So I went and bought a Zac Dawson badge.'

The Western Derby holds a special place in Glenis's heart, a help to her as she delicately navigates the Monday morning bragging rights after derby games with Eagles co-workers. 'I'm not a mean person, but you know, you tend to hear from Eagles supporters only when they win, but you don't hear from them any other time. When the Eagles won [in the second derby of 2015] I was getting text messages. If I come in on Monday and Freo have won I always put the clipping up on the cafe wall out of the newspaper, but I don't rub it in. I just keep a lid on it. I'm a decent person. Just a typical Dockers supporter.'

Despite not being superstitious, Glenis says she has had bouts where she has a dialogue with herself. 'Sometimes during the game I kind of think of what I'd give just to win this one. You make little promises with yourself about what you'll do if you can just get over the line.' Like the time Hayden Ballantyne missed the late shot for goal in 2011 that resulted in a one-point loss, when Glenis had fingers and toes double crossed. 'I do love those close games though. Like the late goal from Longmuir when he kicked the goal after the siren against St Kilda. My son threw up in the car all the way home he was that excited, but I didn't care, I was so happy.'

JANET PETERS – EAGLES

It was a bugger of a week for Janet Peters. Work at the Northam Hospital had been tougher than usual after a virus spread through the place. People were dropping like flies, or were off sick. The temporary staff who had come in to replace the sick were inexperienced, which only exacerbated a difficult situation. As it got closer to the weekend things only seemed to get busier. Janet ploughed on. At three pm on Friday afternoon in July, Janet clocked off and headed home for a quick shower. There were kids to organise and she was due to rendezvous with friends who headed down to Perth regularly to watch the football during the season. The mood was buoyant and once the family hit Midland it was Hungry Jack's for the kids and then quickly on to Subiaco Oval. They had done it so many times it was second nature. The banter and smiles from the kids was a natural tonic that kept Janet's fatigue at bay. They got to their usual parking spot and then headed up the road. Subiaco Oval's lights flickered on, and the butterflies in their stomachs grew. Collingwood were in town for a rare appearance. As they got to the gates there were a few test blasts of the Subiaco siren. They got to their seats and the teams ran out onto the ground. The crowd roared in Janet's ears. She looked around the oval, which was filled to capacity with blue and gold. She smiled and sat down, rubbing her hands together. She sucked in the cold night air and exhaled. 'C'mon Eagles!' she yelled at the top of her lungs as the siren sounded, and the difficult week became a distant memory.

Janet has worked at Northam Hospital for over thirty years, and has lived in the town since she was eleven. It's only now that she's considering a move to Perth where her children live and she can attend the football more easily. For Janet, the Eagles are her first football love. 'I was a part-time follower of East Perth but I didn't really follow football until the Eagles came in. I never went to any WAFL games at all.'

This ambivalence endured despite her parents both being staunch followers of the WAFL. 'Mum was West Perth and she followed football for years and my dad has been a South Fremantle man forever.' Janet does however remember when she was first bitten by the football bug. 'It just became big news when the West Coast came into the VFL. My husband Alan started following and then I started getting interested. Then I had a couple of friends who I worked with: Kate and Annette. They were into football and I guess I just picked it up from them and I started following the Eagles. We all worked at the Northam Hospital and we started going down with our families. It was such a good day coming down and we'd get to the gates and all run to get a good position because there was no set seating – it was just first in, best dressed. If we lost, coming home we'd bag the umpires and turn on the radio and listen to all the comments. We'd always have fun.'

Janet also recalls when the Dockers first came into the league and what she thought of them. 'I didn't dislike them to begin with. We'd just won a grand final and they were mouthing off, "We're going to beat the Eagles, we're not scared of them," and everything like that. Please! A bit of respect. At that first derby I kept thinking let's go out and kick their arses. Which we did many, many times. It was fantastic. You almost felt sorry for them in the first game, you really did. It was the last time I felt sorry for them.' Janet laughs heartily at the memory of the good old days when West Coast reigned supreme and lorded it over their purple cross-town rival. This was a situation that became somewhat more delicate as her father switched allegiances. 'Being a South Freo man when the Dockers came in, Dad actually said, "Look I think I'm going to follow the Dockers, because of the Bulldogs." I mean come on! And after the first season he just said, "I can't do it. I'm an Eagles man."'

Going to the football is a release after the pressures of Janet's job, but it is more than that. 'I just love it when the season comes. I can't explain it. I love going to the football. There's something about getting ready and going to the football and when you walk in, the atmosphere. It's just ... fantastic. I make sure I've got my scarf, the one I've had forever-and-a-day. I used to wash it when we lost to try and wash the loss out, but it's getting a bit tatty and old so it only gets washed at the end of the season now. Things change, like there is a guy down the front of us, and we have seen him grow up. Now he's married with a kid.'

Having witnessed so many Eagles wins early has sealed who Janet's favourite Eagles players are. 'Well you always think of Johnny Worsfold don't you? Those sides in '92, '94 were awesome. Jakovich, we loved. We thought he used to bend over specifically for us, you know. The way he'd run up the wing bouncing the ball. What a champion. Then Benny Cousins came in. Our midfield were very exciting, the best. Now we all love Nic Nait and Joshie Kennedy. I think now they have got a really good team and in the next couple of years it is going to be exciting. But 2006 and the years before were unreal.'

Despite these great players, Janet always suffers from nerves in the lead-up to the derby, conceding that this has everything to do with Fremantle's recent years of derby success and the ribbing she's suffered in her workplace. 'You want to win against the Dockers a bit more than any other side. I'm not as pushy as Dockers fans are. They really like to put it in your face. There was one situation where a lady at work started going on, "Don't you just hate it when Eagles supporters leave when they know they're going to lose." I walked around the corner and said, "Oh don't start – that happens with all sides! When you've got a few little trophies in the cabinet, then come down here and let me know." It went very silent and she turned around and walked out. I would never go down into another area and shoot my mouth off. I do have one person that sits next to me and she puts the Dockers scarf over the chair if they win, and I do it if the Eagles win, but it's all good-hearted.'

Despite some of the recent losses the Eagles have suffered at the hands of the Dockers, Janet remains upbeat and sticks to the rituals that get her through the games. 'Over the last many years we've dragged ourselves to derby games knowing that we're probably going to lose, but we always buy a cake to have at half-time. Most times my friend Kate will bring a vanilla slice, you'd think she'd try to get something different but she doesn't. Vanilla bloody slice all the time. I always buy something different. It keeps my energy levels up as I like to jump up and down and I'm quite vocal. I always say I've done a hard day's work at the football.'

CARLA MACKESEY – EAGLES

Moving interstate in 2005, Carla Mackesey was only a few hours into settling into her new digs on the Gold Coast when the diehard Eagles supporter headed out to have a gander at the new street that she would be living on. The lawns and houses were all well maintained. A lawnmower could be heard in the distance and a few doors up a man was washing his shiny Commodore on the lawn. The sun beamed down and a gentle breeze helped settle her nerves. She closed her eyes and sighed. It had been a big move. She opened her eyes and something caught her gaze: blue and yellow streamers. Mackesey's heart jumped. Perhaps her fears of being a sole AFL fan in NRL heartland were not so justified after all. Right in front of her were the colours of her beloved West Coast. It was finals time, after all. She was delighted and raced inside to tell her husband Andrew, a pilot for Virgin, the good news. 'Andrew, Andrew, you'll never guess, there is a West Coast supporter just down the road. I have to go down and introduce myself, invite them up for a drink … Can you believe it? A West Coast supporter!!' But Andrew gestured for his wife to come over to the table where he was having a coffee. He pointed to the back page of *The Courier Mail*, and the captain of the Townsville Cowboys dressed in navy and yellow. Carla slumped down next to him and placed her head on his shoulder and let out a groan.

For Carla the trip east came about after the demise of the iconic carrier Ansett. 'I was a flight attendant and when

Ansett went under in 2001, my husband got a job with Virgin so we moved to Queensland and the Gold Coast. I had two small children so I stopped flying. When my children were little no one played AFL up here – it was all rugby and soccer – so trying to find AFL teams for the kids to join was really hard. I can proudly say I've got every one of my sons' mates playing AFL for Palm Beach Currumbin Lions. Go Lions!'

Football has been a huge part of Carla's life ever since she was a little girl growing up in the western suburbs of Perth. It was her father's influence that saw her follow the Perth Demons. 'We used to go with Dad. Mum never came because she probably needed a break. We had our little matching tracksuits. All the kids would yell out, "Mick Rea, all the way!" We'd sit there and shout and eat a pie and have a choc milk. Then we'd get bored and go and climb the trees. We'd buy a cooked chook and come home and watch *The Winners* and sit in front of the heater. That was our childhood – that was how I grew up.'

Following the Demons led to Carla's first serious football crush. 'I had a bit of a love affair with Peter Bosustow. It's why I followed Carlton. He was the bee's knees. I used to have Peter Bosustow pictures on my wall – that's how bad I was. After he came back from Carlton I remember we went to Lathlain oval. I was in my teens and Dad introduced me to him. I was beside myself with excitement and then he smiled at me and he had hardly any teeth.'

Once the Eagles came into the VFL, Carla bumped Carlton to her second-favourite team. 'I remember one day getting pulled out of school by Dad and going to the State of Origin game in about 1983. Robbie Wiley played and I remember just loving the whole State of Origin thing. So when West Coast came a few years later it was just complete parochialism.'

Carla's work with Ansett gave her an excuse to exercise that parochialism, as they were the official carrier of the AFL at the time. It also gave her a chance to observe other teams as they shuttled from city to city in the newly formed national competition. 'It would have been in the '90s, and the Lions were on board and the Scott brothers were having a bit of a bender on the way home. They got absolutely belted so they were probably commiserating a bit. It was interesting to see how certain teams reacted, and how West Coast was a very professional outfit, especially under Mick Malthouse. They weren't allowed to drink at all on the way home from matches. They'd have to get up and walk around the plane and stretch. They had huge meals and they got extra leg room.'

When the Dockers came into the national competition, Carla wasn't tempted to switch sides. 'It really was the big brother–little brother syndrome. I mean we were very patronising towards the Dockers – it was like, "Oh aren't they cute, they're trying hard but they're crap." They were no threat at all. Derbies were like another game we were going to win, and we always did. They were never any threat until the Demolition Derby – that was the turning point. What was a friendly rivalry turned into a downright dirty rivalry after that. 'Before the Demo Derby it was, "You're no good, you're not going to be anything," again that patronising mentality, and all of a sudden they became a threat. What was fun banter turned into banter with a bit of an edge to it. Now in the lead-up to the derby I get the text messages and at first they're all very polite. As the day goes on they get snider and then downright dirty sometimes. Sometimes some of my Dockers girlfriends won't talk to me for a couple of weeks. I get so tense in the lead-up but when that first innocuous text comes through, it's game on, because when we lose I'm the worst sport in the world. If we're down by a hundred points I'll sulk. You should have seen me after the 2015 grand final. It wasn't pretty. I have been known to throw things to the other side of the room. I don't like my friends ringing me – I hate that. I want to be the one saying, "Sucked in." I want to be the bad winner – I don't want to be the bad loser.'

Did any of Carla's friends or family switch allegiance to the Dockers from the Eagles? 'My brother did, which is pretty heartbreaking. He's the principal of Mount Hawthorn Primary School and he flies the Dockers flag at school. He'll have purple haze day where the kids have to wear purple to school. He's an idiot. On the other hand my brother-in-law is a bit of a fence-sitter. He has memberships for both the Eagles and the Dockers. Listening to my sister who's been members of both teams talk about the difference in supporters is interesting. Where they sit with the games, there are the West Coast chardonnay-sipping snobs and then the Fremantle ferals. She reckons the chardonnay-sipping snobs are probably more badly behaved than the Fremantle ferals.'

For Carla, the rivalry with the Dockers needs to be put into context, starting with the very first Eagles premiership in 1992. She recounts being with her good friend Susanna Castleden, now a Dockers fan. 'I just remember that day so clearly. Susanna was there when the Eagles won that flag. We drank VB as we watched the replay and cheered every kick and every goal. She should thank me for that because if she had not been an Eagle she would not have experienced the thrill of winning a grand final. In fact a lot of Dockers fans should thank us, as they were probably barracking for West Coast and experienced what it was like to win a grand final, because since then they haven't.'

Despite the humour, recent derby history means that the games are increasingly harder to predict. 'You just can't pick who's going to win. Someone will be sitting fourth or fifth on the ladder and someone will be sitting thirteenth on the ladder but you still can't pick who's going to win. That's interesting, because that's like a final. For example, the second derby in 2015 was like that, and even better because we won. It was a telling derby because it set the finals up for us, because we were considered to be weaker than Fremantle for a while. Fremantle were the contenders and I think that derby set us up; we went, "Hang on, maybe we are a chance." Although, saying that, I wouldn't want to play Fremantle in a derby grand final. No way. I mean, it's bad enough losing a derby, and it's bad enough losing a grand final, so to lose against Fremantle in a grand final: that would be a tragedy.'

LESLEY THE VOODOO LADY – DOCKERS

It was the twin forces of Cyclone Tracy and the Royal Australian Navy that saw Lesley the Voodoo Lady first clap eyes on a new code of football. Having been schooled for years in the mythology and wonder of the West Adelaide Football Club, she found herself in the stands in South Coogee in Sydney. What she saw was unlike any game of 'footy' she had ever seen. The self-described 'under-tall' Aussie Rules fan could not work out why the entire two teams were lining up to take the ruck from a 'throw in'. Then one of the players got the ball and ran like hell as a heaving, sweaty mob chased him like a pack of hungry dogs to the other end of the 'oval'. Lesley asked around and was soon told that this 'game' was not the game she loved but was in fact rugby union. When she moved to Western Australia on Melbourne Cup Day in 1980, her confusion evaporated as she was back in a state that played 'real football'. Her beloved Dockers arrived on the scene in 1995 and the genesis of her magic powers started to grow. It is here in Perth and on the flanks of Subiaco Oval that Lesley administers the dark arts of football voodoo. Having spent all week during the football season bedecked in purple and drinking from an Aaron Sandilands two-hundred-game commemorative coffee mug, Lesley pulls from her bag her secret weapon: Fred the voodoo doll. With an individually made opposition guernsey that Fred wears at each home fixture, Lesley also has a full pack of toothpicks which she strategically places over Fred's body while chanting things like, "Only points, only points," as she lines up Mark LeCras, as he lines up for goal.

Lesley's football story began in South Australia. 'I grew up in Adelaide, virtually at the West Adelaide Football Club. My mum was associated with West Adelaide and was the first lady to get life membership at the club. My grandfather was a sprigger for the under-eighteens, my father used to be the water boy and my brother played for the thirds in those days. We used to have footballers come and stay at the house. The first one was Dexter Kennedy who was just over seven foot high and I used to have to clean his boots. We had to have a special bed brought in for him. He came down from Port Augusta and he went to high school with my brother. We used to get up at five o'clock in the morning and go to the grand final in Adelaide. We'd sit outside the gates in those days and wait for them to open. So yeah it rubbed off with the Dockers, you could say.'

After making the move to Western Australia, it was at State of Origin games at Subiaco Oval that Lesley was introduced to a familiar anti-Victorian parochialism, although she came to her love of the South Fremantle Football Club almost by accident. 'I walked around Freo, I went to the markets and I found Fremantle Oval and I thought, "Right, I've found a footy oval, South are my side."' Football in the state changed forever with the advent of a national competition in 1987, and Lesley was able to see the next tier of football regularly from the lofty confines of the corporate box of her employer, well-known local seafood company, Kailis Bros. 'I worked here in Fremantle for MG Kailis Group for twenty-one years. When the Eagles first came into being, it was a chance for me to go to the football every week. Mr Kailis had a box. I didn't barrack for them but I went because I could see football – that was my main aim. Then when the Dockers came into being he had a box for both the Eagles and Dockers. With Eagles matches you would have to put your name in a hat to get selected. But my girlfriend and I got to go to every Dockers game because nobody wanted to go and watch them because they kept losing. He was a very nice boss, Michael Kailis, even though he barracked for the Eagles. He was definitely an equal opportunity employer.'

But being in the corporate world was not easy for Lesley. Due to their excitement at games, Lesley and her girlfriend were constantly told to curb their enthusiasm, which was at odds with the way they engaged with the game. So they decided to ditch the corporate scene, and head down to the great unwashed, and they have never looked back, having secured excellent seats right on the northern flank. Lesley's passion bubbles up when she recalls some of the derby games witnessed from her membership seats over the years. 'The very first victory where Tony Modra thumped and thumped the ground, that was the best. The Demolition Derby, when Kickett thumped the little weed Phil Read was also memorable. Pity we can't do it now. We [Dockers] are not allowed to so much as touch them [Eagles], or they get a free kick. Ballas only has to breathe on them and he's reported.'

Lesley takes a few deep breaths and has a sip of water and begins rattling off Dockers players who she has enjoyed watching over the years. 'You know all the *under-tall* players are the ones that I liked the best. I've loved Paul Haselby and Jeff Farmer definitely. I've got a picture of Jeffrey on my wall at home. Shauny Mac epitomised Fremantle – he had all the injuries, he was the heartbeat of the club until he retired.' Lesley's love of all things purple is confirmed by her dislike for the 'chardonnay set'. 'The Eagles are the ones that always think that football's about the money. They were set up as a state team and they have got no time for anybody else, and every time we beat them they bring out the same old phrase:

"How many premierships have *you* got?" Please! I tell them to go and watch Foxtel History Channel because that's where their games are on high rotation. It really irritates me. When I was working at Kailis I used to wear Fremantle gear to work every day. I'd have my Dockers flag up at work and when I retired the boss gave me a sign that said A MAD DOCKERS SUPPORTER LIVES HERE. I used to give them hell at work. You've got to show support no matter what they say, whether we win or whether we lose. You take it on the chin but they [Eagles supporters] aren't able to do that.' Lesley stops and leans over the table and looks over her shoulder and back to us. 'It's funny but we've only got one wooden spoon. Same as them.'

It seems incredible that such a diehard, one-eyed Dockers supporter would consider letting any West Coast person anywhere near her, let alone into her house. But the football gods are devilish creatures, and they decided to play a trick on Lesley and her voodoo. 'When we first met our future son-in-law, Wayne, all we talked about was cars. We never got into football. He was a Holden man and that was all we discussed. Then one day he dropped it like a bombshell, and I nearly died. I didn't know he barracked for the Eagles until after he and my daughter were married. When I win, I stick the boots into him and vice versa. He is a bugger; I have sleep apnoea, and he stirs me up all the time saying he's going to reverse the polarity on my CPAP machine. But I've got my way because my two grand-daughters are Dockers supporters. One loves Nat Fyfe and the other loved Tendai Mzungu.'

Which brings us to Fred, Lesley's voodoo doll and how he came into being. 'Well, Nadia Mitsopoulos from the ABC dobbed me in. There's a group of us that sit together at the football, and I try to do something at the beginning of the year that's different. So one year I turned up with Fred, without anything on him, and it didn't work very well. So the following week I put the opposition's guernsey on him. We played Essendon and we won. So then I had to bring it again, and I've been doing that now for five years. In the first derby of 2015, every time the Eagles went to kick for goal I was sitting there saying, "Nothing but points, nothing but points …" and they kicked seven points. It works well, but the trouble is people get in your way. Trainers get in your way and it doesn't always work. If it's not working up to half-time, Fred goes back into the bag. I didn't need him much in 2015; I didn't have to bring him out until the finals.'

Lesley demonstrates how she inserts the toothpicks in the doll as she casts her spell via a cryptic football incantation. It is both alluring and unsettling. We ask whether Fred prepares differently for the derby games. 'At home Fred sits on my balustrade. I put on that week's opposition guernsey. I usually don't say anything to him unless it's a derby. I sit there in front of the television and keep repeating, "Nothing but points, nothing but points." If I'm watching the Channel Seven news and they bring on Ross Lyon I sit there and chant, "You can't out-coach Ross, you can't out-coach Ross," and stuff like that. And everything in my house is purple. I've got t-shirts, I've got underwear, I've got purple fingerless gloves so I can still write the score down. I have purple in my hair and I have my fingernails done in the red, green, white and purple. I've got seven scarves to choose from and I've got four Dockers mugs to choose from, like Sandy's two-hundredth-game mug. On game day we always catch the *second* train from Mandurah, except for Friday games. We come into the city and then get on to a Fremantle-bound train and go to West Leederville and walk to the oval. Fred is tucked in my bag and so are the toothpicks, ready for use when the game starts.'

JEFF NEWMAN – EAGLES

Sitting across from Jeff Newman in the Eagles boardroom, it's impossible not to feel anything other than positive. It's not just the fact that he has one of the most familiar faces in WA, or that his dulcet tones remind us of the gentler times of our childhood. Times when staying up and watching *Telethon* marathons, which he hosted for many years, were the highlight of the TV year for many. But it's something less tangible that makes the previous Eagles number-one ticket holder beam with an inner light. Perhaps it is the smile of a winner. Or because we're sitting in safe Eagles territory where he has been part of the woodwork for so long. Interestingly, for a man who has met some of the biggest stars in the world such as John Wayne, Whitney Houston, Roger Moore and the King of Pop, Michael Jackson, he is, on face value, completely devoid of ego, projecting instead a confident, reassuring disposition, despite the fact that one of his fondest memories on his West Coast journey is getting a black eye from Ernie Dingo. '2006 was a magnificent grand final and I was lucky enough to be in my second year as number-one ticket holder. We had beautiful seats, and I had my daughter and my wife there. I was sitting next to Jack Cowin from Hungry Jack's – they were the main sponsors of the Eagles in those days – and when the final siren went we jumped up and hugged each other. Ernie Dingo came bounding up behind Jack and threw his arms around him and clipped me a ripper across the eye with his hand unintentionally. It was the first ever black eye I've had in my life, and later that year Ernie came across for *Telethon* and I told him about it, and he said, "You should have clipped me back, Jeff, because nobody would have known if you gave me a shiner."'

Jeff came to his love of football in tragic circumstances, after the death of his father. 'I became a fan of football because my dad died when I was eight. Peter, my brother, Mum and I lived in South Perth and we became fans of the Perth Football Club. I played for South Perth as that was in the Perth catchment, and we used to go to the WACA when it was the Perth Football Club's home ground. Wonderful days of Ern Henfry being coach and you were allowed to go into the rooms. There you'd see the footballers and they'd rock in with their Gladstone bags, they'd sit down there and have a fag. They'd pull their shorts on, get a bit of a rub down and then pull their teeth out. In those days you rushed for your seat at Subiaco for the finals because there was no fixed seating. After the game you could run out and grab a sweaty autograph off a player like Merv McIntosh. It was fantastic.'

Jeff goes on to list favourite players like Bobby Coleman, the Harper brothers, Dickie Walker and Barry Cable. 'Gee whiz, there's a story. Barry Cable was probably the best footballer I've ever seen. Ron Joseph from North Melbourne rang me up when Cabes came back from Melbourne and asked if we could look after him. I had a company called Farrell Newman that managed a few people, and I said of course. Barry was one of the first fully professional footballers. We got him some endorsements. He'd walk into the office and he'd be bouncing a ball with this hand and then he would fire a handpass into you that would knock your ribs through to your backbone. Some days we'd go across from our offices on Kings Park Road and play kick-to-kick with Barry Cable, Denis Marshall, and Phil Kelly. Doesn't get any better that. Broke my heart when he came back to East Perth and they won that premiership.'

But with the coming of the West Coast Eagles, Jeff's heart was mended. 'The premierships are all different but they're equally important. I think winning the first grand final was special. It was my wife's first AFL game. She came from Sydney and wasn't an Aussie Rules person. We'd been there ten minutes at the game and Don Pyke gets knocked out by Gary Ablett. I had compered the Eagles grand final breakfast at The Glasshouse in the morning. It was electric. Then in 2006 we ran down onto the ground, Nissie [Trevor Nesbitt, Eagles CEO] got some passes to get us down on the ground and that was probably the most wonderful feeling of my years with the Eagles: being down on the ground and looking back and seeing the crowd of blue and gold still cheering, the song pumping out. I didn't have to compere the dinner that night, so it was great, I could have a few quiet ones.'

Supporting a team with such a winning culture, Jeff's opinions towards the Eagles' cross-town rivals are relatively benign, even where the rivalry has been fierce. 'I think the game that epitomised the players' determination and the feeling with both teams was the Demolition Derby of 2000, which Fremantle won by one point. The derbies certainly aren't, like some have suggested "just another game". East is East, and West is West and never the twain shall meet. It's bloody Fremantle, for Pete's sake. I've got the utmost respect for Matthew Pavlich, for example, who I think was a champion. Modra was great. Sandilands has been fantastic. The little Mayor of Mandurah [Ballantyne] does some good stuff. He only needs to play five minutes each quarter and, like Rioli, gets three touches and kicks two goals. But in saying that, I think we have the best theme song in the

AFL competition. There's no doubt about it. And maybe we should have been called the Perth Eagles instead of the West Coast Eagles because of the Freo thing. But you can't go past Woosha and the first derby where he was the captain and he went out there with a point to prove and he followed through. He was particularly rough, Woosha. Dean Cox has been tremendous and I also think Glen Jakovich has stood out because he was just so good. So reliable.'

Another reliable feature of the derby games for Jeff has been the enduring rivalry between himself and Channel Seven colleague Alison Fan, who in his own words is 'a diehard Docker' and, unlike himself, is quite superstitious about following Fremantle. 'Ali Fan's one who is superstitious. She'll sit in the same seat and she won't get up in case a couple of goals are kicked and the opposition come back. I don't have superstitions like that because it's beyond my control, unlike my golf handicap – I control that.' Saying that, Jeff has had plenty of bets with Alison Fan on the derby games. 'With Ali we have had some great rivalry over the years. Ali is passionate but I've won lots of wine in the early derbies – remember we won the first nine. Many Dockers fans did seem to place more importance on them than we did. So we have had a bottle of 389 [Grange] or something like that over time. Poor old Ali. I went across in 2013 for the grand final, I was compering an Eagles function. I said to Alison, "Let's meet for coffee," so I met her at Federation Square and there she is: purple boots, purple stockings, purple skirt, purple sweater coming towards me. I really wanted them to win but the players let Ross Lyon down. Although I'll make this prediction: if Fremantle can maintain their intensity and their playing ability then they'll be playing the Eagles in a grand final one day. Because the Eagles are going to be there, I can tell you that now. I went to Jack Darling's engagement party in the summer and I was talking to Adam Simpson and I said, "What's the answer? What are you going to do?" He said, "All I want to do is to get them to believe in themselves," and he has done that. He's got Gaff believing in himself, he got Wellingham believing in himself. Brad Sheppard, by geez he's turned into a good player.'

Despite the derby tally nearly being equal, Jeff is obviously feeling confident about the future. As we part, he holds out his hand, and puts it on the line. 'I'll bet you now a good bottle of red that we win the first derby next year.'

LES EVERETT – DOCKERS

Arriving at Les Everett's home just up the road from the Christian Brothers College in Fremantle and down the hill from John Curtin College of the Arts, we expect to be met by the gruff impatient yap of his beloved schnauzer Frankie. To the uninitiated it can be quite unsettling, given her stern gaze and bushy eyebrows, but this soon gives way to a general indifference as Frankie ambles back to her bed for a few zeds. But on this occasion, and to my amazement, Frankie is nowhere to be seen, or heard. Everett, Dockers board member (2003 to 2006), historian (*Fremantle Dockers: An Illustrated History*, 2014) and Goldfields football afficionado (*Gravelrash: 100 Years of Goldfields Football*, 1996) arrives at the door taciturn and seemingly myopic. He raises his eyes and shrugs his shoulders, making it clear to me that Frankie's faux-agitation has given way to mere indifference. Everett's love for his dog knows no bounds and he has even started a blog called talkingfrankie.com – check it out.

Part-time teacher, excellent amateur photographer and lover of good music, food and wine, Everett is no sashaying Freo flunky. Add to that he is the son of a Boulder butcher and in another life a lead singer in a band specialising in country and Elvis covers, aptly called The Everett Brothers, and you might begin to scratch the surface. Les's knowledge of the game is wide, and his love of the Dockers is as staunch as anyone we've met. 'Over time, football has become one of the most important things to me. It is a bit glib, but I know at the beginning of every footy season I'll sit down and start watching a game and I'll think, "I love this." Even last week I went down to watch Peel playing South Fremantle at Fremantle Oval in terrible weather. There were probably no more than three hundred people there. I thought to myself, "I wouldn't want to be anywhere else." There's something about the game – it's unpredictable, changeable. I understand it and I'm seldom happier than when I'm watching a game of footy.'

Les came to football by way of supporting East Perth, on the insistence of his older brother, Dean. 'I think my first year of footy obsession was 1964, when I was nine. Footy cards were everywhere and you collected them from service stations. Dean had a box of footy stuff. There was an article about Alec Epis, a Boulder boy, who had gone to Essendon. There were also articles about Polly Farmer, Ted Kilmurray, Derek Chadwick and other Royals so it was East Perth for me. I listened to the football on the radio, I read papers, I looked at photos; TV didn't come to the Goldfields until 1970. I knew everything about East Perth and just about every other team in the WAFL. But the first players I saw were Goldfields players. Mines Rovers like Ted 'Punter' Robinson, Bruce Weir, and Allan 'Hummer' Spence were my heroes. Punter Robinson had a magnificent torpedo punt but with a Phil Krakouer jam-down kicking style. Then there was Allan Kennedy, one of six Kennedy brothers who played for Mines. He took the best high mark I've ever seen.'

Perhaps Les's allegiance to the Dockers and resilience in the face of their initial lack of on-field success came about because of his support for the long-suffering Royals, starting with the first East Perth game he saw, the 1967 grand final. It was a loss to Perth due to a scintillating performance by Barry Cable, who won the Simpson Medal that day. 'East Perth lost four consecutive grand finals, '66 to '69. They lost it again in 1971. I know pain in football, I'm not a football supporter with a silver spoon in my mouth. But it didn't hurt that much in 1967 because I was seeing my heroes like Syd Jackson and Derek Chadwick, the great number twenty-two for East Perth, for the first time.'

Asked why he never became an Eagles supporter, Les doesn't mince his words. 'I haven't had a moment of wanting to be on *that* bandwagon. I was actually overseas for a few months in '87 and came back and the season had already started. The footy landscape had completely changed. I went to a WAFL game and couldn't believe that there was no one there. Listening to the radio, there were West Coast's general managers and other administrators all banging on about the bloody Eagles. I didn't like the idea that, being a West Australian, I was meant to barrack for West Coast. I didn't have a VFL team. I almost became an Essendon supporter because of Derek Kickett, but dropped them on grand final day in 1993. So I was ripe to take on this new outfit but they just didn't appeal to me.'

Asked to name his favourite Dockers players, Les pauses while Frankie lazily walks over and stretches herself out in the late winter sun. She raises a bushy eyebrow, like she already knows Les's answer. 'I really loved Dale Kickett. There was something wholehearted about the way he played for Fremantle. I always knew he was a good player but at the AFL level he hadn't quite proved it. But I think at Fremantle he did. I was really pleased when I saw him at Fremantle's first training run on the thirty-first of October in 1994 at Fremantle Oval. It was a real privilege watching Matthew Pavlich from the start. He was a player of such quality for so long. I was pleased Fremantle got Michael Johnson. I remember that he came down to train for the club to try out for a rookie spot. He wasn't selected. I was very keen on him coming to Fremantle, and to see him and his career develop has been tremendous because things haven't come easy for him. Nathan Fyfe is a glorious player and Son-Son Walters makes me smile.'

For Les, the derby is an interesting beast that offers a chance to beat the 'mob up the road', but can also leave a bitter taste in the mouth. 'I kind of dread derbies. I'm glad when they're over, I can't stand it. When West Coast win any game, it has a double, quadruple effect when they beat us on the rare occasion. I don't look forward to the derbies particularly, and I've been known to avoid them if they're away games. I remember once I was in a record shop buying the new Bob Dylan album a few years ago. It would have been 2007 so maybe the album was *Modern Times*. I ran into a bloke I used to work with, a North Melbourne supporter, and he reminded me the derby was on. He said, "Don't you follow the footy anymore?" He was buying a Bob Dylan album as well – *Blood on the Tracks* from memory. I ducked into a butcher's shop after that and looked up at the TV on the wall, and Ryan Murphy scored a goal. I got home and did not switch on the TV. Then finally that evening having had dinner and listened to the album I somehow found out we won, so I watched the replay. If we'd lost it's quite possible I would have just ignored the game. Like the 2006 grand final. I haven't seen any of it. It's immature but I just can't stand derbies.' This all came to a head one year when Les bumped into Eagles coach, the late Ken Judge, after the biggest ever Eagles win in a derby in 2000. 'I was at the shops at South Fremantle on the Sunday and Ken Judge was walking in and I stupidly said, "Your boys were pretty good yesterday, Ken." Of all the people you don't want to run into it's the coach of the opposition. That day I should have stayed home.'

It was the Dockers' first derby win that is Les's fondest memory. 'I was in the press box, and it was an away game for us but by the last quarter the game was all but over, and Fremantle was going to win. I remember the great Freo supporter Matt Price from *The Australian* saying quite loudly for everyone to hear to Stocksy of *The West Australian* [Gary Stocks, now West Coast Eagles Communications Manager], "So how many of these Eagles do you reckon would get a game with the Dockers?" There was no response from Stocksy. Word was that he'd had a wager that West Coast would win the first ten derbies. They won nine. The big bet had almost come off. Since then, the derbies are an even bigger deal if you take into consideration all the history and bullshit that has gone into them, the players, the drama, the wins. It's a pity those great Freo players like Paul Haselby who would always play well in derbies weren't able to play in a grand final. Aaron Sandilands is a huge performer for the Dockers in derbies. For me, Sandilands has been the most important player. The Eagles have allegedly had all-Australian ruckmen in Naitanui and Cox, and yet they never beat Sandilands, never. Then I think of other games like when Sandilands had his jaw broken and Graham Polak rucked and we won it. I do think that one day there will be a derby grand final but just who will win it I don't know. I might not find out for some time if I'm in Freo shopping for cutlets or a Dylan album.

'The game itself would be really weird, and it would be an incredible scramble for tickets and flights and all that sort of stuff. But if I couldn't make it to the MCG, for some reason, it would be very interesting because you'd have all the Dockers supporters, half the city, down in Fremantle, and the other half would go to West Coast, wherever that is.'

LUC LONGLEY – DOCKERS

It is some time in 1998 and the Chicago Bulls are flying back home in a private jet from yet another win against some hapless opponent in the NBA. The most recognisable person on the planet, Michael Jordan, is gently dozing in an expensive recliner. Scotty Pippen and Dennis Rodman are joking around with one another, and Luc Longley has both of his knees strapped in ice as he sits back and samples some of the sponsor's product. As the beer works its magic, Longley reaches into his backpack and pulls out a VCR tape and asks one of the team gofers to put it on the plane's video system. A smile immediately comes to the Chicago Bulls centre's face. Before long, several of Luc's team mates have gathered around and are asking him questions about the game. Even Jordan is awake and checking out the hits and the marks of this game Luc calls 'footy'. As the game rolls on, Luc's enthusiasm for the Dockers doesn't wane despite the flogging they are getting at the hands of the opposition. All of a sudden the video recording stops, and the screen turns to snow. The players turn around as, from the back of the plane, the Bulls coach Phil Jackson begins to give the Bulls a concise speech to the effect that if they want to continue on with their winning ways, then watching and rooting for teams that are losing isn't on. Jackson handed the tape back to Luc and the big man acknowledged the coach's point. For now, he'll have to wait until he gets back to Chicago where he can watch the team he loves in the comfort of his own home.

We sit down with Luc inside the Fremantle Dockers' headquarters at Fremantle Oval, not far from where he grew up. 'I grew up on Cliff Street down underneath the Roundhouse. There were no kids around that part of Freo at that stage, only old drunks and old seafarers and the occasional hooker. So Freo was kind of my playground and what I used to do on a lot of weekends was come and watch South Freo play, especially if there was a game between South and East Fremantle. Stephen Michael was a real favourite growing up and Maurice Rioli was obviously pretty handy. When I brought my kids back from America in 2001, one of the first things we did was come down here to Fremantle Oval to indoctrinate them into being a West Australian. Now when it's derby day I've got an old scarf and an old beanie that I wear around. On derby day I tend to get a feed at the markets, a crepe and wander around.'

Luc Longley's connection with the Dockers is inextricably linked to the Indian Ocean and the Dockers inaugural jumper. 'Before basketball and girls, it was the water for me. I bought a tinnie when I was ten and I used to get around the fishing boat harbour in it and try and scab stuff off the fishermen and catch fish. Like, I thought Freo was me. It was my identity. Then while I was playing basketball in America I became a Harbour Master member and went to the launch and I was presented with the jumper. I loved it. The anchor on the jumper, the nautical thing, it was a no-brainer. The red and green I thought was a stroke of genius. For all of its shortcomings and the symbolism, the anchor was awesome. And I've got a theory about the clash of strips. I think the Dockers chose purple because it looks so bad against blue and yellow.'

Luc's history as a professional sportsman allowed him to take the long view when it came to the Dockers' early years of struggle. 'I love this winning culture now and what we're doing, but back then the way I saw it was that the rare wins are particularly nourishing, especially when you don't have many. I didn't mind that we were struggling for everything. I think it's part of the DNA of the club, and of Fremantle too, in a way. I'm not an Eagle-hater but I feel like the Eagles are kind of the big brother that we try to out-muscle, or the twin we're trying to differentiate ourselves from. When there's a derby it really is the perfect storm. We're sometimes lucky to get the opportunity to have a really loaded game, and I imagine that, at some point, the last game of the year will be a derby.'

So how did Longley explain football to his team mates in the states? 'I didn't even try to explain what footy meant to me because they were not the audience to do that. I did try and explain the game, and the rules, which is actually really hard. I just gave them some very broad basics. In the end, what the guys like Jordan and the others liked watching most was the mark of the year, and the goal of the year. The tackling, the hits and all that sort of stuff. They loved a speccy. They really appreciated the courage and endeavour of the footy players, but also some of the hardships of playing when compared to elite American athletes. Some guys over there can get a little bit insulated and wrapped in cottonwool, like, "My bag wasn't delivered to my room in time." So seeing the footy players running backwards into packs and taking marks and just bouncing up and keeping going really impressed them.'

As a Fremantle boy, it was a natural thing upon returning home for Luc to fantasise about playing for the Dockers. 'I had this little dream of coming back and playing for the Dockers. I figured I could do it before the body really broke down. That would have been so much fun. And as far as derbies go, I guess that I value them because we don't have a lot of real traditions in Australia. We've got the dawn service on Anzac Day, and the Blessing of the Fleet [ceremony in Fremantle] but really we are pretty short on cultural traditions. With the derby, it is that ceremony that I suppose I like as much as the game itself. I usually gather a bunch of mates at my house. I hired some scaffolding once and made a grandstand inside my house. I always try to create a bit of an event around it. That for me is the cool part – trying to build that cultural legacy.'

For Luc, the derby rivalry is all about the way the fans and members engage with the match on game day. 'Yeah, I always thought Australian crowds are a bit rawer and a bit more emotional than the NBA crowds. The NBA's like a BMW, it's almost like a silent idle, they can perform if need be whereas an AFL crowd is like a lumpy camshaft that sounds like at any moment it's going to explode. Derbies especially: they are as close to finals as we can get, I reckon, and it brings out the best in players. I always loved Luke McPharlin just because he's so dour and he's got a cool name. Who doesn't love Son-Son? I used to love Troy Cook and Grover just the way he crashed and banged. The Wiz also, but Cookie was my favourite. I am also a fan of Aaron Sandilands – I like watching him play a lot.'

Derby day also means partaking of Luc's regular bet with another basketball success story. 'I have an ongoing bet with Andrew Vlahov. It's hard to have a bet with him because he is like a low-calorie beer kind of guy. I'm not. We came to an arrangement where if Freo wins, he pays me floor to ceiling boxes of proper beer. If the Eagles win, I pay him floor to ceiling boxes of something sensible. No one's ever had to pay up yet, but I'm sure one of us will be on the phone to the other pretty soon.'

BILL SUTHERLAND – EAGLES

Bill Sutherland meets us at the Eagles' headquarters at Subiaco looking a bit worse for wear. He has some very distinctive, fresh grazes on his face. He explains he has been fighting bushfires down at their farm in the Stirling Ranges, deep in the Great Southern of Western Australia. He came incredibly close, he reckons, to becoming yet another victim of the increasingly vicious bushfires that have been ravaging the state's south over the past years. But the greatly respected West Coast Eagles trainer is tough and wily, and he smiles and touches his forehead as he recalls in vivid detail the journey from country footballer to becoming the head trainer for the West Coast Eagles from the period of their inception to his retirement in 2007. 'I was a trainer with Claremont before I joined the Eagles. I went to Singapore on a cruise, and the Claremont Football Club was on the same boat. Before that I was an East Perth supporter. The Claremont people asked me to come down to Perth, as I was living in Dowerin and farming, and join them for a few drinks at the club. The head trainer at Claremont got in my ear, and let me sit on the bench alongside the other trainers to watch what they do, and before I knew it I was doing it.' Billy Sutherland soon built up a reputation as one of the best trainers in the WAFL, and when the Eagles were born, he offered to help. 'I was president of the WA Football Trainers Association at the time, and I said to Mossy [Graham Moss], "If you want a hand in selecting the trainers for the Eagles, I'll give you a hand." We leased our farm to the next-door neighbour's son, and I became an applicant for the job and got it. We had one trainer from Perth, one from Swan Districts, a couple from West Perth and Subiaco, and all these blokes had different ideas of how to do things. It was quite intimidating for me to put this all together, and deal with footballers from other clubs. I had to store all the gear in our garage at home. I couldn't even put one of my cars in there. They paid me five thousand dollars and took fifteen hundred dollars tax out. It was a lot of work for a little money but other support staff were not getting a lot either and incidentally nor were the footballers of the day. I had every injury recorded from day one. Robert Wiley was our first, he pulled a calf on the sixth of January 1987. They were paying me a modest sum until Michael Brennan and a couple of the boys got together and went to the hierarchy and said, "Look, we want Bill full-time."'

Bill's memory for detail is acute, and those first few away games seem like yesterday. 'Claremont fans are a bit like Eagles fans – they just sit there and clap, whereas you'd go down to West Perth and they're likely to tear your heads off. They really hated us in Victoria. One day we played at the MCG, and the kids had those little containers of milk, like the ones you get on planes, and they were pelting us with those bloody things.'

It was that early baptism of fire for the Eagles team that coloured his perception of the Dockers when they entered the competition in 1995. 'We went through a fair bit in the early stages, and I think our fellas felt as though we were competing for sponsorship and allegiances, and we could see this other mob coming in and pinching that. We'd think, "Well, they don't really deserve that, we'll sort this mob out when they get in here," and we did.'

It was through the trading of players that Sutherland

was able to get a greater insight into the mindset of the Fremantle Dockers. 'When Trent Carroll and Greg Harding joined us from Fremantle they reckoned the whole Dockers preseason was taken up with how they were going to beat the Eagles. Premierships weren't discussed. In those early days the dislike between the two teams was verging on hatred. Some of the players that they had weren't top players, they'd done nothing, but were really good at mouthing off. They'd kick a goal and run around the boundary like soccer players high-fiving the fans and all that sort of crap.'

This was in stark contrast to the quiet relief Bill felt after the Eagles won their first grand final in 1992. 'If you watch the video of that first premiership, the siren has gone and everyone has got up. Mainwaring leapt up with a busted leg, and I'm just putting my water bottles back into the holder. I just sat there for a while before going out onto the ground. It was more a relief to me. I went to the back to the hotel and sat in my room and drank a stubbie of beer.'

Back in the West, it was important from the first derby that the Eagles made a statement of how things were meant to be. 'The first derby was pretty brutal. Our blokes went in pretty hard and that was an organic thing. There was no instruction beyond *just don't get reported*. I recall that the build-up was pretty intense. I remember we played Fremantle in a really low-key thing down at Fremantle in the preseason and they beat us, and Malthouse's two boys did not want to go to school on Monday, because the other kids were going to give them some screw over this win. I remember that first derby very well. I remember the brutal way our players went out that day. They were like a mob of dogs that've just been let off the leash and they hit the Fremantle players with a bang. No one held back. I think those hostilities in those early days were brought about because the Eagles had been going for a bit, and we were the big boys, and I think some of our players thought these Dockers blokes had done nothing and were trying to challenge us for a mantle that we'd earned. Then the fans quickly got involved and you know, some of their fans are very vocal.'

It wasn't long before the importance of the derby was realised to players of both teams, particularly as the contest became more even. 'I remember they beat us in a derby that we should have beaten them in. Ben Cousins come into the room and put his head in his hands and said, "Bill, we couldn't beat this mob of bastards in a game of marbles." After one game Mitch White came into the room and apologised for letting the Dockers beat them. Talking to Mark LeCras a while back, he says if he played for Collingwood in the Anzac Day game, his feelings would not be the same as playing for the Eagles against Fremantle. The feeling would not be as intense. Now, because of the trading of players from both teams, and with players coming from different parts of Australia, I think there isn't the same intense feeling about the derbies as there was then.'

Bill had an inside view of the build-up to the derby games. 'The week before the game it would kick in as the media started talking about it. You could see it in the back of the players' minds. It hit fever point a few days before as the tension grew. The feeling was more like the preparation for a final. But we trainers just treated it exactly the same – it was just business as usual, although it was different for the players. Chris Judd was always the complete professional and always gave a hundred percent. Ben Cousins loved being with the boys and loved the challenge. But I think Brett Heady really shone in derby games. He took it very seriously. Brett Heady was overshadowed by Dean Kemp and a couple of the other players that were really shining at that time. But Brett was a great footballer and the derbies is where he starred.'

Now that he's retired, does Bill miss the games, and the derbies in particular?

'I wasn't ever wild about football itself. I got more enjoyment out of watching Cousins, Judd and some of the lesser players achieve success. I never missed a game in twenty-odd years, and I think the hardest part for me was when they flew over East for the first time without me. If I miss anything in football, it's when I see them running out on the oval and I'm not with them.'

JOHN PRIOR – DOCKERS

It was 2013 and experienced barrister John Prior was quietly going about his preparation in the lead-up to the Dockers qualifying final to be played in Geelong. He thought about going over, but the switch of venue from the MCG to the newly refurbished Kardinia Park saw Prior reconsider. In the end, staying at home seemed like a much more sensible option than heading over to Victoria and the hostile Geelong crowd. As he messed around doing odd jobs and menial household tasks, the time to bounce-down got closer and closer. He showered and got dressed and headed into the lounge room. He opened a can of soft drink and took a long swig. The doorbell rang. It was several of his son's school-mates. He could not recall anyone being invited or intending to come but he asked them in anyway. No sooner had he seen that group in, then the doorbell rang again. More of his son's friends arrived, then another lot. The lounge room quickly filled. Prior called his son Tom over. 'So what's going on here? I thought I was just watching the game with you and your brother. Are they all Dockers people? I know for a fact that kid with the red hair is an Eagles member.' Prior's eldest son Tom smiled. 'Dad they've all come to watch *you*. You are the entertainment.' As a game, it was a dour struggle but then late in the fourth quarter Stephen Hill, who was coming off the bench and unmarked, got the tap down from Sandilands and raced off and kicked the goal that saw Fremantle get into the 2013 grand final. Prior was out of his seat weeping with joy as the lounge room erupted, including the red-headed

West Coast supporter. As Prior recounts this story, his eyes well up with tears of happiness, because when it comes to the Dockers and their decades of struggle, John wears his heart on his sleeve. Asked to describe his own journey with football, he leans over to his bookcase and hands us a book. The title is *The Green Machine: An Anecdotal History of the University Football Club: A Drinking Club with a Football Problem*. He chuckles at the title. 'For me, I love the fact that football crosses all generations and all walks of life. I go out to people in prison all the time, and the first thing they want to talk about is the footy, not about whether they're going down for twenty years. As for myself, I played junior footy with Steve Malaxos. He said that I'm the worst footballer he ever played with. I was the most enthusiastic footballer, perhaps, and I have great knowledge of the game, but I just can't play. But I do hold a record. I was playing F-grade for university and I got dragged at quarter-time. I came back on at half-time and kicked seven goals in the second half. Two were relayed free kicks, and the rest were what I call *Joe the Goose* handballs over the top. My job was to hang around the boundary, and as the ball came down everyone ran out, and I'd stand in the goal square by myself. Get a cheeky one over the top and straight through the sticks.'

John also coached local junior sides as a means to earn extra cash while he was studying law at UWA. 'Coaching the under-thirteens juniors I used to get something like eight hundred dollars for the season. I barracked for Claremont as a kid because I grew up in that area, and lots of my mates were good footballers who played for Claremont. Then with coaching we had some Claremont champs playing in the juniors back in the day like Tony Evans and Don Pyke, and Ben Allan was also floating around.'

It's the mention of the two future Eagles players that draws an admission from John. 'Look I'm a bit ashamed to say this, but I did barrack for the Eagles when they started, because I always saw them as the state team, and I have fond memories of State of Origin. But as soon as Freo started I said, well I live in the southern part of the metropolitan area and I had that Claremont connection through Gerard Neesham. So following Freo just seemed to make sense. I was working in a firm called Talbot Olivier, and Paul Olivier, one of the partners there, was heavily involved with East Fremantle, so when Freo started they said, "Well, do you want to do the legal work if the players get in trouble?" So I've been involved in Fremantle since the start. But I actually reckon I was getting bored with the Eagles' winning culture, and that notion of entitlement. The "we rule Perth" sort of thing. As much as you hate the Melbourne teams, all the winning was putting me off. I'm a person who always goes for the underdog. I also have this problem that West Coast Eagles supporters never understand. Clubs are tribes, and Fremantle is a suburb. When Fremantle win the flag we all know where to go. Where do you go when the Eagles win? Do you go to Joondalup or Rockingham? I don't know. Geelong is a place. Collingwood and Port Adelaide are places. West Coast is a concept. Also, I've always admired the ability of Indigenous footballers, and Gerard Neesham knew how bring out the best with Aboriginal players. Indigenous players can do things that white men can't do.'

Looking around Prior's office it's hard to believe that we're actually in a barrister's office, rather than a football museum or clubroom. Framed jumpers and Freo footy knick-knacks are all around, many of them signed gifts from footballers John's represented over the years. Can he explain to us what the journey with Freo has been like? 'Well, it's been a bit of a roller-coaster. A colleague of mine was not going to renew his membership a few years back, saying it's all too hard with

Freo. I said, "How will you feel when we win a premiership?" I don't think Eagles people get that because they've had success so early. I tell my kids I don't care if I'm connected to a whole lot of tubes, you take me to the MCG if we're in it. If I'm dead you can put my ashes in a box and take me in a box. And as far as derbies are concerned, I think it's an absolute furphy that the rivalry is seen by some as being confected.

'I know the Eagles mantra is "When are you Dockers going to get over this derby obsession?" We've heard all that. The stuff I get from Eagles people when they win against us is tenfold of what we do. Clearly we were a joke in the beginning, they had a state side in 1992 and 1994 then in 2006 there was what I call "the taint". The truth is that derbies are different. They are definitely different to other games. I know coaches love to say it's just another game but the players I know are more candid. I think the derby rivalry's great for the state. It sells newspapers; it gets people talking around the water cooler; judges have got something to talk to you about instead of boring old court cases. I remember vividly having lunch with Matthew Carr, telling me about the infamous derby where Matt and his brother Josh, at the bounce-down, got stuck into Cousins. Josh won the Glendinning Medal and got the pie thrown at him. Matthew said, "I will never forget the look in Josh's eyes before the ball was bounced when he was looking at Cousins and [Daniel] Kerr."'

John's derby rituals are straightforward. 'I always go and put a hundred bucks on the Eagles before the derby. People think I'm an idiot. It's my pain insurance. I don't care what the odds are, because if the Eagles win I just go, "Well, those bastards bought me a free dinner." And if Freo win, I'm happy with the win. I see it as a donation. On game day my wife will not let you bring chardonnay into the house, because that is an Eagles drink.'

So who are some of John's favourite players and derby moments? 'Scott Chisholm I loved. One minute he'd do something brilliant, the next minute he'd bounce the ball and it would go over his head. He was winning the Brownlow halfway through the Brownlow count in the first year, and no one knew who he was. The Wizard, Jeff Farmer. One of the most talented footballers I have seen. I've got a soft spot for Clive because my good friend, the late Matt Price, has his chapter on Clive in his book *Way to Go*, which is fantastic. That's what kept us going through the dark times. Andrew Wills hugging the crowd, Plugger [Tony Lockett] running down the field trying to catch Stephen O'Reilly at the WACA. Justin Longmuir kicking a goal after the siren against the Saints. But the most important statement in a derby was when Shaun McManus got poleaxed by David Wirrpanda. McManus was a warrior – he wasn't the greatest skilled player, but he *was* the club, I reckon. And then there was Tony Modra's iconic goal. And when Dale Kickett hit Phil Read and he got the relayed fifty and kicked the goal. People forget that we won by one point, so it wasn't the eleven punches that he laid – it was the goal he kicked that won us the game.'

When asked whether or not there will be a derby grand final, John becomes expansive. 'Look, you would have to say yes. There is lots of WA talent coming through and both sides are strong at the moment. It would be bad for Melbourne, as it would be all West Australians at the G. Perth would be deserted. I mean, it's a bit like that on grand final day anyway but it would be times ten that. There'd be blokes in my industry who'd been picked up that night in the dock at the Magistrates Court on Friday, sitting in the dock on Saturday, and there would be no magistrate, no prosecutor, no one.'

CLIVE MERCER – DOCKERS

As the proprietors of a Fremantle institution, Mercer Cycles, it's customer loyalty that both Sally and Clive Mercer have worked hard to foster. In contrast to Sally's easygoing nature and bubbly personality, Clive is a seemingly shy and retiring person, but with a sharp, dry sense of humour. To understand the types of businesspeople Clive and Sally Mercer are, one has to go back deep into Clive's memory, back to when he was a baby in Ipswich, England, where the central actors were his parents Geoff and Joan, who opened their first bike shop in 1946. The story goes that one night a cyclist sustained a puncture while riding. A passing police officer stopped, and the cyclist asked where the nearest bike shop was, so he could repair his mode of transport. 'The policeman told him go and down and see Mercer's,' Clive deadpans, 'only problem was that it was four in the morning. Anyway, this guy is standing there throwing stones up against the window to wake my dad up, which he did of course. We lived above the shop, where I was actually born in 1955. The stupid thing is, Dad woke up and came down and fixed the bike, probably didn't even charge for it.'

As a boy, Clive was mad for Association football (soccer), which took up any spare time he had. 'The amount of time I spent up the recreation ground in England was huge. It stays light for longer there, so after dinner I'd head up to the pitch and there'd be twenty or more guys up there playing soccer.' Moving to Perth in 1971 Clive discovered that the car was king and the racing was not that great, but he loved the weather and the lifestyle. Attending Rossmoyne Senior High School, Clive continued to play soccer in high school and beyond. 'I ended up playing second division in the State League, which was pretty reasonable, we just kept winning divisions and going up.' In 1973, at the age of eighteen, Clive got a quantity surveyor's job with the Public Works Department.

Mercer Cycles in Fremantle was opened in 1979 by Clive's father, Geoff. By then Clive was bike racing. The retailing seed sown back in England was further nurtured by time spent in the shop. 'My dad and mum worked with Malvern Star throughout the '70s. My mum died in January 1977, soon after dad became state manager with Peugeot Cycles Australia. But they shut down the WA branch after he'd been there about a year and left him high and dry. When he was fifty-nine and he had no job, he decided to open up this shop. So basically at my age now, he started a shop from scratch. I was twenty-four at the time. Soon after he opened, I left and took off in March 1980 to the UK.'

Clive spent most of the '80s in the UK enjoying himself. 'I got my job and I was playing soccer and I was bike racing. I headed back here for trips. I helped out when I was here to give Dad a break.' It was soon after that Clive and Sally decided to move back to Perth. 'I'd been working with Dad since 1990 and Sal came in full-time about 1995, just after the kids were born.' But in 1999 Geoff Mercer decided to drop a bombshell on the young couple. 'It was about five o'clock and we have half an hour to go on the thirty-first of December 1999, and he says, "I'm going to retire at the end of the month." I'd been thinking about the possibility because we'd been making him cut down hours over the years, so I think he was only working two or three days a week then, but then he told us, "I think I'll retire in half an hour's time." He gave me thirty minutes notice before retiring and we had to choose and so we took over the shop.'

Clive became interested in football through a fellow student who was playing in the WAFL at the time. 'I'd seen it at school but I didn't really understand it, to be honest. One of the guys I went through quantity surveying with at WAIT, which is now Curtin, played for West Perth, so I picked things up a bit from him and even did the football tipping as well.'

It was from this grounding and after the advent of the Eagles that Sally and Clive started to engage more with AFL football. 'We watched the Eagles on TV if they were playing, and you'd want the Eagles to win and support them. We got upset in the grand final that they lost in '91 to Hawthorn at Waverley. We were interested, but not overly, because working at the shop you never got much time to watch it.'

When the Dockers entered the competition in 1995, the club made themselves known to the local bike shop owners. 'One guy by the name of John Rankin from the club was coming into the shop regularly. He used to be in the SAS and helped with the Dockers training. It was a bit all over the shop because Freo didn't have a whole heap of money, but they needed stuff fixing in the gym like the bikes. So we would go down, fix the bikes in the gym for them, because they're local and just down the road, and then wait six months to get paid. We also got paid in signed footies, posters and a guided tour of the clubrooms.' Clive laughs at this memory but it was through that connection that his interest in the new AFL franchise began to take shape, in the form of a football club that seemed to align with the struggles Clive's father faced all those years before, when he opened the shop for the first time. 'The Dockers I think suffered more than the Eagles, because the Eagles got off to a good start. No one really wanted the Dockers to come in, and they didn't get a whole heap of help. The Eagles got a team that was almost like a State of Origin side. It's probably the reason I started to identify with them because Dad opened the shop up on a shoestring, but it's grown since then, which I can relate to with Freo.'

So from this understanding, does Clive think that the rivalry between West Coast and the Dockers is real or confected? 'Absolutely real, not just the build-up and the hype. It is a bigger game and you probably get carried away with the hype. Like we used to have Ina Giuffre down the road who owned the deli, she's an Eagles supporter, so every time we went in there to get some milk or a paper we'd stir her up and she gave as good as she got. We had a standing bet with Ina – a two-dollar scratchy. I felt sorry for her because at that time we were just killing them every time, so I hardly had to pay out. There are quite a few people in Freo who have stayed Eagles supporters, and the Eagles are clearly our biggest rivals. You always want to win the derby because otherwise you know you'll get shit from the delivery men if you lose. And lately our form has been pretty good, so several notable people have kept their mouths shut. You always feel that when Freo lose, the media have a good bite out of the Dockers. Old George Grljusich gave them a hard time, but it's the Eastern States commentators, they have a view that is very stereotypical that Freo are losers, and you wonder, did they even see the game?'

Clive's favourite derby was the first one of 2015, because 'during that first half you never heard so many Eagles supporters go so quiet. It was fantastic. They were just like rabbits in the headlights.' However, this moment of pleasure was in stark contrast to that moment a few years earlier, 'when Ballas had that kick after the siren and hit the post. It was so weird – like there were a couple of seconds there when you felt great, and then you found out that it was a behind. It was a split second of pleasure, then a world of pain.'

Given the proximity of the shop to the Fremantle Oval, are any Dockers players regular customers? 'One of the best ones was a visit once from Matt de Boer, Alex Silvagni and Jon Griffin. It was a really busy Saturday morning and my daughter Sara's fixed her favourite Docker, Matt de Boer's, puncture. Luke McPharlin comes in a bit to get his bike fixed up, as did Brett Kirk when he was a coach, Sally's favourite, who bought bikes for his kids, which was good for business because he has five. They are just really nice, and they're not up themselves or anything, so you just chat. It's a pity my favourite has never come in. I loved the way Jeff Farmer played; he was a showman and people used to give him heaps. He was what you go to the football for.'

MARK GREENWOOD – EAGLES

Mark Greenwood is an author with a passion for history. His books *The Legend of Moondyne Joe* and *The Legend of Lasseter's Reef* won West Australian Premier's Book Awards for Children. *Ned Kelly and The Green Sash* won the West Australian Young Readers' Book Award, and *Simpson and His Donkey* was a Children's Book Council of Australia Honour Book and an USBBY (United States Board on Books for Young People) Outstanding International Book. Mark has also written children's books on Aboriginal history such as *Jandamarra*, and the recently released *Boomerang and Bat* – the story of the first Aboriginal cricket team to tour England in 1868. He is married to Frané Lessac, a wonderful naive painter. Their historic Fremantle home, as you would expect of two well-established and travelled artists, is like stepping into a gallery.

Greenwood smiles and opens a bottle of shiraz, pours out two glasses, sits down and takes a sip. He's more than happy to talk about the West Coast Eagles – but with the qualification that his love of football came originally from his allegiance to the WAFL team, East Fremantle. 'My father played a few league games for the Perth Demons and the Claremont Tigers. He won a best and fairest in the seconds with Claremont, but he was always an East Fremantle supporter. As a little kid I use to tag along with him to East Fremantle oval and watch the games there. Old Easts had so many great players – David Hollins, Brian Peake, Gary Gibellini, Graham Melrose and Freddie Lewis, just to name a few. I used to wear number eight on my jumper, which was Freddie Lewis's number. He was the guy with slicked black hair, who could kick a big droppie from outside the centre. Freddie was just a gem and a really fair player. I grew up in my blue and white jumper, and played junior footy for East Fremantle, then Ardross and Attadale, as well as for my school. Football has always been a big part of my life.'

These formative football experiences have forged lifelong friendships that still endure today. This generally means Mark and his childhood mates gathering at one another's houses to watch the West Coast Eagles and sample some bourbon. 'Our tastes have matured. We started off with the Jim Beam. Now it's Maker's Mark, Buffalo Trace and G.W. Dant. But the thing that has remained the same, over all the years, is that every winter weekend the footy brings us together! Everybody knows where their seat is. It's pretty blokey.'

Mark has been a loyal fan of the Eagles since their inception, despite growing up in Fremantle and continuing to live there. 'I was a West Coast fan from the day that they came into the national competition. I would have found it very difficult to jump ship and change my allegiances, as others did. I couldn't. And my passion for derby rivalry stems from those epic games I watched as a kid between South Fremantle and East Fremantle. I see the Eagles–Dockers rivalry as an extension of that football history.

'I've always believed that, from its inception, the Fremantle Football Club should have united derby rivals, South and East, under one banner so that they could have continued their historic legacy in the AFL. I don't know why they didn't merge the rivals' colours – which started out as the Imperials and the Unions and became East and South Fremantle. Red, white and blue are the colours of Fremantle football history. If the great rivals had been united from the start, I may have been tempted to support the Fremantle Football Club.'

Mark's identification with the Eagles was forged by his admiration for some of the West Coast's favourite sons. 'There are so many great players in the club's short history. I really admired Chris Mainwairing. Mainy was a great team man. I met him outside of footy, through people who knew him in Geraldton. He was a terrific person and a really tough player. Matera, Kemp, Woosha, Bluey … and the underrated players like Tony Evans and David Hart – so many great players. Don Pyke, Jakovich, Cuz, Kerr. I remember seeing Chris Judd playing in a preseason game and telling my dad, "I've seen someone really special. He just had something about him."'

Mark pours another two reds before moving on to the topic of the derby games. 'It's more than bragging rights isn't it? The derby is a celebration of a classic football rivalry. It's an extension of the football I remember when I used to go to those South Fremantle and East Fremantle games with my dad. The derby's divisiveness brings West Australians together because we all share a love of the game. We enjoy a contest. Of course it's painful if you're a Dockers fan and they lose a derby. It's the same for Eagles fans. But those experiences unite fans and that is the great thing about the derby. It pulls us apart. It brings us together. It's always historic. A derby bounce-down always puts the hairs up on the back of your neck. I reckon that is why the derby means so much. The emotional core of football is captured in derbies – it's the beating heart of West Aussie football. When I go to a derby and hear Dockers supporters chanting "Freo! Freo!" it drives me nuts. But it tells me the rivalry is real – the passion is real – and it's game on!'

For such a hardcore Eagles man, Mark hasn't been lucky enough to have witnessed any West Coast grand finals and, despite their history of success, he's unsure as to how he'd feel about a derby grand final. 'It's a nightmare scenario for both sets of fans. There would certainly be some anxious people around – myself included. Over the years I've learned you can never count the Dockers out. Even if they're behind on the scoreboard, they have an uncanny ability to fight it out – and win. That makes me uneasy. If there ever was a derby grand final, imagine the build-up. All that West Australian football history distilled into the biggest game of the year. We got close to that scenario in 2015. A West Coast Eagles versus Dockers grand final would be a very scary thought for fans of both clubs – but I'd have to be there!'

JULIE & ADRIAN HOFFMAN – EAGLES

We meet Julie Hoffman and her eldest son Adrian at their Palmyra home. Julie has spent all day at a rally to protest the government's planned Roe 8 highway extension, which would see the road pushed right to the back of the Hoffman family home. Understandably she is riled up that her home is in jeopardy. They are, however, both used to adversity, being Eagles supporters who live in Fremantle. Adrian provides a cool and calm contrast to his mum as he is well-known around the port city as the lead man of some Fremantle-based indie bands, The Morning Night and Marley Wynn. He has also played as a guitarist on occasions with the re-formed Triffids and Steve Kilbey.

After the rigours of her day protesting, Julie opens a bottle of red and her mood softens as she speaks of her love of football. 'My grandfather and my dad were both very big South Fremantle supporters. Grandad lived in Hamilton Hill most of his life. The only thing to do on a weekend was go to the footy. You'd get your little bucket of chips and can of Coke and off you went. I absolutely loved it. The dirty big marks and the beautiful goal. It was the atmosphere that was great.'

As his mother speaks Adrian smiles and nods his head. His reply is very similar to his mother's. 'I love the Eagles because my parents were mad Eagles fans, but the love started when Dad took me to East Perth games as a young kid. It was like a day with dad, ice-cream, chips and gravy and a kick at half-time, and I think after a few years of that I probably started to take notice of what was actually happening in the game and I fell in love with it.'

For Julie, the uniting of her personal world and her allegiance to the Eagles came about on her wedding day, after she'd just become a young mother. 'We didn't have a lot of money back then, and Adrian was only a baby. Shaun, my husband, said to me, just pick a date and go with it, so the twenty-sixth of September sounded good. Then it dawned on us the closer it got. The wedding was two o'clock in the afternoon. The Eagles won their first premiership that day, and that's when my love for them was born, on the day I got married.' Julie goes on to mention that two years later her best friend picked the first of October for her wedding day, the date the Eagles won their second premiership against Geelong.

Adrian's faith in the Eagles was cemented by his admiration for a particular player. 'Benny [Cousins], mate – he made me want to play football. He was the first player I really fell in love with. I kind of saw him as superman when I was a kid. A superhero that could just do anything and save the day. These days it's Priddis – he's my new favourite player. Mr Reliable. Ben has given him his cape.'

Julie had a different favourite. 'Ashley McIntosh stood out for me. He wasn't the superstar, he wasn't the super good-looking one, but I liked him. I remember when Adrian was only young and going out to the Thornlie shopping centre, and Dwayne Lamb was out there and I was in awe of him. He was a favourite also.'

Asked whether, being Fremantle people, they were tempted to switch allegiances when the Dockers were born, Julie looks as if I've broken a family heirloom and Adrian just chuckles. Adrian responds first: 'As a muso can I officially say about the Dockers: shit song, shit colours. Despite the fact that I love Fremantle as a town and Fremantle is my favourite place in the whole world, I could never go for them.'

Julie can actually pinpoint when she understood that she would never go for Freo. 'I won a prize at a quiz night and it was a Dockers jacket. White, green, red and frickin' purple. I'm just thinking, "What bloody football team has these colours? – they are just too embarrassing for me to wear." I actually held onto it for a couple of weeks but I couldn't do it. I gave it away. I mean, who picks those colours?'

Asked which derbies spring to mind as memorable, Adrian doesn't hesitate. 'What made me hate the Dockers for a while was the big derby punch-up in the Demolition Derby. As a young kid when you see a fight against people you love and respect, you just think, "You dirty bastards, how dare you."'

Julie nods in agreement. 'I don't go to derby games because I would seriously need a medic next to me. I find myself yelling too much. Come derby day I'm better off sitting by myself on the lounge or doing a bit of cooking. I'll pop outside and water a couple of plants and look over at the telly now and then. One recent example was the second derby in 2015, a game that I knew we were going to win. I'd gone over to my sister-in-law's a couple of days before the game. She is a one-eyed Dockers member and could not make the Dockers home derby. She offered me the tickets as they are really good seats. The day before she dropped the tickets off, a bird shits on my car right on my West Coast sticker. It was a good luck sign. I knew from that moment that we were going to win. I didn't go to the game but when we won I was just sitting back on the lounge thinking, "Okay, Dockers, get your shitty purple jumpers off." I went out the front of the street and you could see all these purple balloons. I let out a huge "Go Eagles!" at the top of my lungs.'

To which Adrian adds, 'and the sound echoed through

Fremantle!' He recalls coming home on the train that evening with his father Shaun, and popping into the North Fremantle Bowling Club to watch a local gig. 'I love my Eagles scarf, I always wear it proudly for derby games, and we got off at North Freo station after the game. We went to the bowls club and it was packed out with Dockers. That's the greatest thing. Sticking it up 'em when we were not expected to win.'

Mother and son disagree however on the importance of a potential derby grand final. 'A derby grand final is my biggest fear,' Julie says. 'I just simply could not watch it because I reckon my little heart would explode, the pressure would be that big. Too crazy and too full-on for me. If the Dockers were to win that would just drive me insane. It's bad enough watching the cafe strip being painted purple. I would probably hold a grudge for my whole life.'

But Adrian is smiling and confident. 'Mum can't even handle a regular derby, so a grand final derby would be like the full catastrophe. Me, on the other hand, I would be all for it, and I hope it happens soon.'

PETER MUDIE – DOCKERS

Among followers of the Fremantle fan site Dockerland.com, the handle of 'Pollyanna' is perhaps the most recognised and respected. As we sit in his studio office at UWA, we remind him of some of the pithy observations of life and the fortunes of the Dockers that the wiry and wily expat Canadian has made on the fan site. In particular, his optimism when it comes to the Dockers is unsurpassed. Also an unabashed fan of Aboriginal players, he is quite possibly the most staunch of all the Dockers fans. So how did Peter become Polly? 'Well, there's always a bit of a question as to whether I'm a man or a woman on Dockerland. It used to be Sussi's handle [Peter's former partner] but she incensed Shane Richmond [the Dockerland webmaster] over something and got kicked off, so I just took it over from there.'

So what is a Canadian doing all the way out in Australia and how did he come to Australian Football? 'I was in Tasmania for a while doing my master's degree at the art school there. I came down in 1983 until 1985 on a Commonwealth scholarship and was fascinated by the Krakouer brothers when they played for North Melbourne. I really got into football via them and used to go and watch North Hobart in the local league. North Hobart Oval was the closest oval to where I was living. Studying and renting a house by myself, as a single parent with my daughter, and being on the other side of the world – what do you do? Winter in Tassie was a pretty tough place for football even just to sit there and watch a game. But on television you can't see the full field and how the play opens up. That is how I came to love footy – by going to the local Tassie games.'

A few years in Darwin helped Peter thaw out, before he headed down to live in Perth. It was here that he took the next step and adopted a football club. 'I've spoken with a lot of people about their heritage and tradition in following political parties, or teams, and in a lot of situations that is something that's predetermined by your family ties or background. But I was in a situation in Australia where I didn't have that history, so I could just make my own mind up on this. But even then I didn't become a paid-up member of the Dockers until the 2000s. What clinched the deal for me was Jeff Farmer – when he came home it made the Dockers special. My favourite player though was Dion Woods. Dion was a master at the game (especially the geometry of evolving play), but with Jeff anything could happen and he was spectacular. It was like the best part of football that I had seen in the '80s put together as a whole unit, and that unit was Freo.'

Asked why he wasn't tempted to follow the more successful Eagles instead of the struggling Dockers, given that he had a free choice, Peter is frank.

'I think that the separation between West Coast and Freo is very similar to the way I feel about Americans and Canadians. For me, Americans, collectively, are a bunch of knobbers. Individually they are lovely people. But Americans exude the kind of privilege that West Coast have always projected and seem to constantly maintain. It was a kind of a class thing I picked up on, but I always knew that we would get on top of the bastards. We will always be better than them.'

Which means that for Peter the biannual derby fixtures are key to demonstrating the differences between the two clubs. 'No way is the derby *just another game*. I hate it when the coaches say that! It's like a cannon shot that goes off and divides the town. It's much more than entertainment, it's more than a sporting contest, it's deeply political. Connolly and Harvey understood this, ask the guys that play and see what they say. Ask some of the derby heroes like Hasleby if it is just another game. Ask Jeff or Des Headland or bloody Kicketty [Dale Kickett]!'

Peter repositions himself on the chair and looks at us squarely. 'I'll give you an example. In 2007, we didn't have a good year and in the away derby that year we were supposed to get beaten to a pulp. I went into Freo to get Sussi's nieces a couple of presents, and Heath Black was in there with his kids. I said g'day and I wished him good luck on the weekend. I didn't think we had a hope in hell. Black looked at me, his eyes were fierce and he said, "We're going to take them, without a doubt." I got on Dockerland and everyone went, "Polly, you idiot, of course that's what he would say." But we won that day when no one gave us a chance. Josh Carr got the medal, it was magnificent.'

Peter didn't have a ticket to this, one of his most memorable derbies, and instead listened to the game live on the radio (instead of the delayed television broadcast), hanging on every kick. 'I could hear it was changing at the end of the third quarter, and knew that we were going to do it. So I had my ute all ready to go. I had my huge Freo flag, I had those magnetic stickers stuck all over the car, the ones that said JEFF IS GOD. I dressed out this old Falcon with all sorts of crap, under-chassis flashing neons and a modified pizza delivery light on the roof. I drove up to Subi during the fourth quarter and when the final siren sounded and I drove around in the usual Subi traffic jam until there was no more traffic that night.' The memory makes Peter laugh, especially in the context of his following of the club through some difficult years. 'In the dark old days where we would get pumped, a good day out at the derby was if Grover (or Belly) dakked someone. The sense of a loss would be less if there was a good dakking, and it kind of made the game satisfying. It's the theatre when you lose that's sustaining, and the more absurd the better.'

With a Derby looming on the weekend, as a fan with an appreciation for the absurd, Peter's preparation for the game and the rituals he maintains during the game are vitally important. 'I don't drink on derby day. It's the only game where I don't have a beer, because your nerves can get on top of you. I try not to think too much during the week until the day of the game. Then I get onto Dockerland and seriously start thinking about football. I start thinking about our injuries, our form and the stats. I have a pair of undies that I only wear on derby day. The elastic's gone, and I've got to wear a belt now to keep 'em up. I always wear the same tricolour jumper with Jeff's number thirty-three. Some other little things I do, but when things go wrong you've got to readjust your compass and do something impromptu. For example, one day after a few drinks at the Irish Club before a game, I remember we were walking along Roberts Road, and we found ourselves in front of the Eagles shop. I said to Sussi, "I wonder if that shop is longer than a human breath." She scrunched her face up, knowing how stupid the idea was. I angled my head towards Subi and started to boo, walking briskly trying to get from one side of the Eagles shop to the other. I've got a good boo and I can really boom it out. I was going hard, when out the door comes David Wirrpanda. He's standing there looking at me like I'm the village idiot, but it's always bugged me that we are renting our home games at Subi – it's seen as the home base of the West Coast Eagles and their corporation. I did it out of irritation; Wirra wasn't amused.'

The thought of beating the Eagles in a derby grand final

gets Peter's juices flowing. 'I know a lot of people think it wouldn't be a good thing, that a loss would be devastating. But we wouldn't lose to those bastards. Straight up, there is no way in the world we'd let that opportunity pass, that opportunity to set the record straight. Could you imagine how good the world would look after pounding those bastards in a GF? I mean just look at the 2015 grand final. Jack Darling did one of the best falcons I have seen, it was better than five dakkings. Also it was a very rare chin falcon, almost as rare as the double falcon. It was more enjoyable than Rioli's goal. I'd risk a heart attack for that absolutely. Just to see Mikey Walters kick the winning goal. He would not miss, the kid is that determined. And just to add a final insult into the Eagles' coffin – Mikey would *torp* it.'

WESTERN DERBIES

	Year	Date	Round	Home team	Score	Away team	Score	Ground	Crowd	Winner
1	1995	14 May	7	**West Coast**	**23.13 (151)**	Fremantle	9.12 (66)	Subiaco Oval	40,356	West Coast by 85
2		3 September	22	Fremantle	8.10 (58)	**West Coast**	**16.15 (111)**	Subiaco Oval	39,844	West Coast by 53
3	1996	31 March	1	Fremantle	6.9 (45)	**West Coast**	**9.13 (67)**	Subiaco Oval	33,041	West Coast by 22
4		21 July	16	**West Coast**	**12.10 (82)**	Fremantle	7.6 (48)	Subiaco Oval	35,406	West Coast by 34
5	1997	13 April	3	**West Coast**	**16.15 (111)**	Fremantle	9.17 (71)	Subiaco Oval	39,294	West Coast by 40
6		3 August	18	Fremantle	7.7 (49)	**West Coast**	**13.4 (82)**	Subiaco Oval	39,711	West Coast by 33
7	1998	12 April	3	Fremantle	10.7 (67)	**West Coast**	**14.10 (94)**	Subiaco Oval	34,710	West Coast by 27
8		2 August	18	**West Coast**	**15.9 (99)**	Fremantle	8.12 (60)	Subiaco Oval	37,145	West Coast by 39
9	1999	28 March	1	Fremantle	13.20 (98)	**West Coast**	**15.12 (102)**	Subiaco Oval	32,680	West Coast by 4
10		18 July	16	West Coast	11.6 (72)	**Fremantle**	**17.17 (119)**	Subiaco Oval	36,763	Fremantle by 47
11	2000	15 April	6	**West Coast**	**28.10 (178)**	Fremantle	9.7 (61)	Subiaco Oval	40,460	West Coast by 117
12		30 July	21	**Fremantle**	**15.11 (101)**	West Coast	15.10 (100)	Subiaco Oval	37,573	Fremantle by 1
13	2001	21 April	4	Fremantle	13.10 (88)	**West Coast**	**16.16 (112)**	Subiaco Oval	38,804	West Coast by 24
14		12 August	19	**West Coast**	**14.14 (98)**	Fremantle	9.10 (64)	Subiaco Oval	41,285	West Coast by 34
15	2002	31 March	1	**West Coast**	**21.11 (137)**	Fremantle	18.10 (118)	Subiaco Oval	39,467	West Coast by 19
16		20 July	16	**Fremantle**	**15.10 (100)**	West Coast	11.4 (70)	Subiaco Oval	41,779	Fremantle by 30
17	2003	27 April	5	Fremantle	10.13 (73)	**West Coast**	**16.12 (108)**	Subiaco Oval	41,654	West Coast by 35
18		30 August	22	West Coast	11.16 (82)	**Fremantle**	**14.12 (96)**	Subiaco Oval	43,027	Fremantle by 14
19	2004	1 May	6	West Coast	11.7 (73)	**Fremantle**	**12.11 (83)**	Subiaco Oval	42,135	Fremantle by 10
20		22 August	21	Fremantle	6.9 (45)	**West Coast**	**13.5 (93)**	Subiaco Oval	41,907	West Coast by 48

21	2005	9 April	3	Fremantle	12.8 (80)	**West Coast**	**12.16 (88)**	Subiaco Oval	42,027	West Coast by 8
22		12 August	20	**West Coast**	**19.4 (128)**	Fremantle	12.8 (80)	Subiaco Oval	40,720	West Coast by 48
23	2006	6 May	6	**Fremantle**	**12.16 (88)**	West Coast	12.11 (83)	Subiaco Oval	42,213	Fremantle by 5
24		27 August	21	West Coast	8.13 (61)	**Fremantle**	**18.10 (118)**	Subiaco Oval	43,527	Fremantle by 57
25	2007	14 April	3	Fremantle	11.4 (70)	**West Coast**	**14.17 (101)**	Subiaco Oval	42,051	West Coast by 31
26		5 August	18	West Coast	14.13 (97)	**Fremantle**	**19.10 (124)**	Subiaco Oval	43,096	Fremantle by 27
27	2008	5 April	3	West Coast	10.13 (73)	**Fremantle**	**12.15 (87)**	Subiaco Oval	39,027	Fremantle by 14
28		3 August	18	**Fremantle**	**17.14 (116)**	West Coast	12.11 (83)	Subiaco Oval	42,096	Fremantle by 33
29	2009	2 May	6	West Coast	9.20 (74)	**Fremantle**	**13.9 (87)**	Subiaco Oval	41,654	Fremantle by 13
30		25 July	17	**Fremantle**	**10.11 (71)**	West Coast	8.18 (66)	Subiaco Oval	39,536	Fremantle by 5
31	2010	2 May	6	West Coast	10.13 (73)	**Fremantle**	**17.9 (111)**	Subiaco Oval	40,886	Fremantle by 38
32		1 August	18	**Fremantle**	**24.16 (160)**	West Coast	13.7 (85)	Subiaco Oval	40,451	Fremantle by 75
33	2011	15 May	8	**West Coast**	**14.12 (96)**	Fremantle	9.9 (63)	Subiaco Oval	40,567	West Coast by 33
34		24 July	18	Fremantle	9.10 (64)	**West Coast**	**8.17 (65)**	Subiaco Oval	41,055	West Coast by 1
35	2012	27 May	9	**West Coast**	**11.18 (84)**	Fremantle	5.6 (36)	Subiaco Oval	40,905	West Coast by 48
36		4 August	19	**Fremantle**	**17.11 (113)**	West Coast	6.12 (48)	Subiaco Oval	39,694	Fremantle by 65
37	2013	23 March	1	**Fremantle**	**16.12 (108)**	West Coast	11.14 (80)	Subiaco Oval	39,629	Fremantle by 28
38		14 July	16	West Coast	14.9 (93)	**Fremantle**	**19.7 (121)**	Subiaco Oval	39,839	Fremantle by 28
39	2014	4 May	7	West Coast	7.12 (54)	**Fremantle**	**11.7 (73)**	Subiaco Oval	40,476	Fremantle by 19
40		28 June	15	**Fremantle**	**13.10 (88)**	West Coast	11.15 (81)	Subiaco Oval	40,490	Fremantle by 7
41	2015	19 April	3	West Coast	12.9 (81)	**Fremantle**	**17.9 (111)**	Subiaco Oval	39,138	Fremantle by 30
42		16 August	20	Fremantle	11.14 (80)	**West Coast**	**15.4 (104)**	Subiaco Oval	41,959	West Coast by 24
43	2016	9 April	3	**West Coast**	**12.20 (92)**	Fremantle	8.11 (59)	Subiaco Oval	40,555	West Coast by 33
44		7 August	20	Fremantle	9.10 (64)	West Coast	**17.8 (110)**	Subiaco Oval	36,215	West Coast by 46

BIGGEST WINNING AND LOSING MARGINS

West Coast 117 points

2000	Round 6	WC 28.10 (178) F 9.7 (61)

Fremantle 75 points

2010	Round 18	F 24.16 (160) WC 13.7 (85)

COACHES

Fremantle Dockers Coaches

Gerard Neesham 1995–1998
Damian Drum (from round 9) 1999–2001
Ben Allan (from round 10) 2001
Chris Connolly (from round 15) 2002–2007
Mark Harvey (from round 16) 2007–2011
Ross Lyon 2012–

West Coast Eagles Coaches

Ron Alexander 1987
John Todd 1988–1989
Mick Malthouse 1990–1999
Ken Judge 2000–2001
John Worsfold 2002–2013
Adam Simpson 2014–

ROSS GLENDINNING MEDALLISTS

2001	Round 4	Drew Banfield (West Coast)
	Round 19	Glen Jakovich (West Coast)
2002	Round 1	Chad Fletcher (West Coast)
	Round 16	Paul Hasleby (Fremantle)
2003	Round 5	Michael Gardiner (West Coast)
	Round 22	Paul Hasleby (Fremantle)
2004	Round 6	Paul Hasleby (Fremantle)
	Round 21	Chad Fletcher (West Coast)
2005	Round 3	Chris Judd (West Coast)
	Round 20	Chris Judd (West Coast)
2006	Round 6	Chris Judd (West Coast)
	Round 21	Peter Bell (Fremantle)
2007	Round 3	Michael Braun (West Coast)
	Round 18	Josh Carr (Fremantle)
2008	Round 3	Matthew Pavlich (Fremantle)
	Round 18	Matthew Pavlich (Fremantle)
2009	Round 6	Paul Hasleby (Fremantle)
	Round 17	Aaron Sandilands (Fremantle)
2010	Round 6	Michael Barlow (Fremantle)
	Round 18	Aaron Sandilands (Fremantle)
2011	Round 8	Matt Priddis (West Coast)
	Round 18	Dean Cox (West Coast)
2012	Round 9	Matthew Rosa (West Coast)
	Round 19	Matthew Pavlich (Fremantle)
2013	Round 1	David Mundy (Fremantle) & Michael Barlow (Fremantle)
	Round 16	Michael Barlow (Fremantle)
2014	Round 7	Lachie Neale (Fremantle)
	Round 15	Stephen Hill (Fremantle)
2015	Round 3	Lachie Neale (Fremantle)
	Round 20	Josh Hill (West Coast)
2016	Round 3	Matt Priddis (West Coast)
	Round 20	Josh Kennedy (West Coast)

CONTRIBUTORS

James Baker and Cath Podger met in The Bird on William Street in Northbridge and were married in 2015. Cath had a mobile upbringing, growing up in Perth, NZ and Tasmania due to her dad's PhD work in Australian plant pathology. James grew up in Palmyra and later played in such seminal Australian bands as The Victims, the Hoodoo Gurus, The Scientists, The Dubrovniks, The Beasts of Bourbon and, most recently, The Painkillers.

The Hon. **Julie Bishop** was born in 1956 and grew up in the Adelaide Hills, and studied law at the University of Adelaide. Since 2007 she has been Deputy Leader of the Liberal Party and has served as the Minister for Foreign Affairs since 2013. She has held the federal seat of Curtin in WA since 1998. She has now presented an Eagles scarf to both a US president and, more recently, a US vice-president.

In the early days of the extended VFL, **Fedele Camarda** remembers being excited by the prospect of a Fremantle Football Club. Many of his friends and family felt the same way. He says: 'While some enjoyed the theatre of WCE and others stuck with their "Winners" team, we were hoping for something of more substance. Something that tapped into the area's rich football heritage and culture that we could easily identify with.'

Maria Camporeale is a high school teacher who has lived in and around Fremantle for most of her life. Growing up as a fierce South Fremantle Bulldogs supporter since moving to Fremantle at the age of ten, Maria found it easy to extend her football allegiance to the Fremantle Dockers when the port city was finally granted its own football team.

Kevin Croon was born on 4 June, 1945, in Lower Hutt, NZ. He attended Rata Street Primary School and Nae Nae College. He left school at fifteen and started his own rock and roll band. For the next six years he worked full-time and also played five to six nights a week in his band. Aged twenty-two, he started his own business, Croon Contractors Pty Ltd. For the next twelve years he carried out many earth-moving projects throughout NZ. In July 1979, aged thirty-four, he emigrated to WA with his wife Levanah and daughter Jacqui. Kevin now owns and operates The Roof & Wall Doctor with his family, and considers himself a very fortunate and very happy Fremantle resident.

Jesse Dart is an East Fremantle born football fanatic. A Fremantle Football Club member for eleven years and an East Fremantle member for twelve, Jesse has grown up in the port city with an intense love of football. He plays as a goal sneak for his junior football team. Jesse's dream is to become a footy commentator, with the ultimate goal of calling an AFL grand final.

Ron Elliott writes novels and for the screen. He has followed the Eagles since the beginning. So do his daughters. He loves all Eagles players but his special era favourites are Dean Kemp, Andrew Embley and Mark LeCras, players with massive hearts who are multiple threats.

Les Everett is the author of *Gravel Rash: 100 Years of Goldfields Football* and *Fremantle Dockers: An Illustrated History*. In his spare time he takes photos of footy scoreboards. Les looks after the websites australianrules.

com.au, talkingfrankie.com and scoreboardpressure.com. He doesn't like derbies much.

Alison Fan is a senior journalist at TVW Channel Seven. Born in Perth, she has worked in the media since 1963 having worked both locally and internationally with the *Daily News*, the *Oakland Tribune*, the ABC and Channel Seven. Fan is perhaps best known for her work around the Perth Mint Swindle, when she anonymously received one million dollars worth of gold. However, her proudest moment came in 1982 when she was the first female reporter to be allowed into the change rooms for the WAFL grand final. She is married and has five grandchildren.

Glenis Freemantle (Hurst) is a loyal and passionate Western Australian and dedicated Fremantle Dockers supporter since their inception. Married with two sons and one daughter, Glenis has spent many enjoyable years of her children's upbringing dedicated to voluntary work in local junior football and netball circles. She joined the hospitality industry in 2002 and spent the last five years happily working as a cafe supervisor at Curtin University.

Maria Giglia has been with the Dockers since their inception, supporting them through thick and thin, and has been part of the Banner Team for eighteen years. She says: 'We have had great times; I've thoroughly enjoyed every moment. It has been a wonderful journey, an experience in itself. Fantastic memories and friendships for life. We have been just like a family spending every Monday night together for six months of the year. We all catch up with each other off-season for coffee or a meal.'

Mark Greenwood is an author with a passion for history. He has twice received the WA Premier's Book Award for *The Legend of Lasseter's Reef* and *The Legend of Moondyne Joe. Simpson and His Donkey* was a CBCA Honour Book and an USBBY Outstanding International Book. Recent titles include *Jandamarra*, which was shortlisted for the CBCA Eve Pownall Award, the NSW Premier's Literary Award and the *West Australian* Young Readers' Book Award.

An information studies academic with a penchant for Scandinavian crime-thrillers, **Gaby Haddow** was the first to pose a question any Eagles-supporting librarian worth their salt would ask: Who's archiving the memorabilia? Over the six years Gaby took on this role, she collected a taxidermied eagle, hundreds of newspaper articles, a jar of MCG dirt from their first grand final, and much, much more – all essential now to the Eagles' history.

Adrian Hoffman is a Fremantle musician. His current band is called Marley Wynn. He has fronted Perth band The Morning Night and been a session musician with The Triffids, Steve Kilbey, and Davy Lane from You Am I. His latest album is called *25 Bruised Boysenberry Ave*. He reckons you should all go out and buy a copy.

Julie Hoffman was born in Subiaco in 1970. She recalls a childhood that was full of memories that revolved around football when she was a Bulldogs supporter. In the mid-'80s, Hoffman left high school and decided that she would pursue a career in pharmacy, which lasted sixteen years. She met her future husband Shaun soon after leaving school and they got married by choosing a random date, September 26, 1992 – grand final day! Thankfully for the newlywed Hoffmans, the WCE won that day, and her love for football was reborn. Julie is now forty-six years old, still married to her best friend after twenty-four years and has three wonderful loving children.

Greig Johnston spent the first ten years of his working life as a guitar teacher, and the next seven as a writer and editor with a strong focus on sport. Born into the cult of Glasgow Rangers Football Club, he also fell in love with boxing at a young age. Now he is happiest sitting in the sunny outer at Subiaco, watching a comfortable Eagles win over Essendon, Karl Langdon and Peter Bell's 6PR commentary piped into one ear.

Justin Lee Langer AM is a former cricketer who represented Australia in 105 Test matches. He is the current coach of Western Australia and the Perth Scorchers in Australian domestic cricket, and has acted as the interim coach for the Australian cricket team. A left-handed batsman, Langer is best known for his partnership with Matthew Hayden as Australia's opening batsmen during the early and mid-2000s, considered one of the most successful batting partnerships ever.

Lesley the Voodoo Lady was born in Adelaide, is a mum of two, and nanna to four granddaughters. She has lived in Crib Point, Hastings, South Coogee, NSW, Waverley Caringbah, Mount Pritchard, Darwin, Cooloongup, Port Kennedy, and Warnbro. She worked for the MG Kailis Group for twenty-one years, Jotun Paints for nine years, and retired one year ago. She enjoys carpet bowls on Wednesdays.

Deanne Lewis was born and raised in Perth, mostly living in the northern suburbs with her mother, grandmother, three siblings and extended family. Deanne is a Yamatji/

Nyoongar mother of two daughters and four grandchildren. Deanne's mother was born north of Perth in Morawa and grew up in the country town during the '50s, but she and her siblings came to Perth for schooling and sport as they were very talented and recognised in both areas. The love of sport was inherited by Deanne, and she supported her cousins at Claremont and East Perth footy clubs, and her brother and her partner, Rodney, down at the old Innaloo Bulldogs club. Like her mother, Deanne studied and gained qualifications in Aboriginal Health and has spent over twenty years working in this sector. She has a passion for the health of her Aboriginal community, children and, of course, the Dockers.

Dennis Lillee AM, MBE was born in 1949 in Subiaco, WA. He is a former Australian cricketer and known as the most outstanding fast bowler of his generation. When he retired from international circket in 1984, he held the world record for the most Test wickets (355). He was inducted into the ICC Cricket Hall of Fame in 2009.

Luc Longley was the first Australian to play in the NBA where he stayed for ten seasons. Playing alongside Michael Jordan, Scottie Pippen and Dennis Rodman, Luc was the starting centre for the Chicago Bulls when they won the championship from 1996 to 1998. He represented Australia at the 1988, 1992 and 2000 Summer Olympics. In 2001, he was inducted into the Australian Institute of Sport 'Best of the Best'. In 2006, Longley was inducted into Basketball Australia's Hall of Fame. In 2009, Longley was inducted into the Sport Australia Hall of Fame at its twenty-fifth anniversary dinner in Melbourne, becoming only the fourth basketball player to be inducted. In 2013, he was named an assistant coach of the Australian Boomers.

Allan (Alsy) Macdonald is a musician, lawyer, and Fremantle Dockers fan. He has also, of late, succumbed to peer pressure and adopted East Fremantle as his local WAFL footy team – not so surprising, since he has lived in that fair town for nearly twenty years. Alsy was a founding member of WA band The Triffids and remained its drummer until the band stopped playing in 1990. He then turned his talent for recalling obscure trivia at will towards getting a law degree while also raising a family with fellow Triffid, Jill Birt. Alsy recalls vividly the unveiling of the new Freo Dockers team colours on the Footy Show (from memory) in 1994, and the ABC radio broadcast of their first game the following year, when they nearly rolled the Tigers at the G. Nothing much has changed for the Tigers in the ensuing twenty years, but Alsy is proud of how the Dockers have managed to turn failure into a virtue, then into success (well, not 2016, or 2001, or 2007–2009 …).

Carla Mackesey was born into a sports-loving family in Perth. She married another sports lover and passed her footy passion on to their children. In 2001, following the demise of Ansett, she and her husband had to relocate for work to the Rugby League state of Queensland where people looked at them as if they were aliens when they said they followed AFL. Fortunately, they are lucky to be able to travel back to Perth every few months where nobody calls footy 'aerial ping-pong'. You know what they say: you can take the girl out of Perth but you can never take Perth out of the girl. Carla's ambition is to stop Queenslanders calling the umpires refs!

Ian MacRae was born and raised in Scarborough, WA. Ian's infatuation with all that is football was first ignited with a new arrival in his street in the mid-1960s. Kevin

Murray, star of Fitzroy and the VFL, was to coach East Perth. Like most aspiring footballers, the realisation that not everyone was blessed with the skills to succeed soon kicked in. This epiphany was not the end, however, but the beginning of a fascination with the game, its structures and its cultures. Saturday afternoons sitting on the grassy banks of Leederville Oval soon progressed to coaching juniors and then ultimately to the hallowed domain of an AFL Club's inner sanctum. The journey never ends.

Ross McLean was an avid footy and cricket player as a younger man. Later on he was the federal MP for the seat of Perth from 1975 to 1983. Later still he was the chairman of the Fremantle Dockers from 1999 to 2001, which Ross describes as some of the toughest years of his life. He has five children and fourteen grandchildren and still supports the Dockers.

Shaun McManus is one of the most popular players to ever represent the Fremantle Football Club. Known for his courage, persistence and resilience in overcoming two knee reconstructions, he has now become a popular Perth celebrity working in both radio and TV. McManus was the co-captain of Fremantle in from 2000 to 2001 and was the second player to reach 200 games with the club. At the time of his retirement, his 228 games was the second highest number of games played for Fremantle behind Shane Parker. Following the retirement of Peter Bell during the 2008 season, McManus became the last remaining player from Fremantle's inaugural squad to still be playing in the AFL. He is married to Meegan and has four children.

Clive Mercer is a lucky man. He has survived two open-heart operations where the odds of survival were one in 100.

In 1991 he married Sally. They have twins Sara and Andries, and they go to all Freo's home games, rain, hail or shine. He is hopeful that Freo will win a premiership one day.

Kia Mippy is a Yamitji woman from Perth. Kia has been a West Coast Eagles supporter from birth thanks to her amazing father who was a great footballer in his time. He originally supported North Melbourne, but switched to West Coast once they entered the AFL competition in 1987, happily passing his enthusiasm on to Kia. Her passion for football developed from an early age – growing up in Geelong around the time of the Geelong–West Coast rivalry. Kia moved to WA in 2006, and is now a West Coast member who avidly watches all West Coast Eagles games. She currently works in the education sector.

Peter Mudie is an expat Canadian academic, artist and filmmaker and is a staunch supporter of unionism, Indigenous rights and the Fremantle Dockers. He has written numerous articles and books on the film avant-garde and has worked under a range of pseudonyms in various contemporary art fields. Since the 1980s, he has lived and worked across Australia and has settled with his family in WA.

Jeff Newman grew up and lived in South Perth where he played football and cricket at school. He naturally became a fan of the Perth Football Club and with his mother and brother were frequent visitors to the WACA, Perth's home ground. He followed the mighty 'Redlegs', and loved such players as the Harper brothers, Reg Zuna and Bob Coleman to name a few. The Demons, as they are now known, gave Newman many happy moments and he felt it was only natural that he follow the West Coast, becoming a 'tragic'.

As a life member of the West Coast Eagles Newman looks forward to many more memorable moments, including a premiership or two, in their exciting future. Go the Eagles!

Gillian O'Shaughnessy has been a journalist with the ABC in Perth for the past twenty years, and currently broadcasts *WA Afternoons* on ABC Radio. She has lived in Fremantle for over forty years, and is passionate, some say borderline obsessive, about the city and her footy club, the Fremantle Dockers. She has proudly tipped them for the flag every year since the club was formed, and remains deeply confident in their inevitable success.

The Hon. **Melissa Parke** was elected as the federal member for Fremantle in 2007, 2010 and 2013, and she retired in 2016 after serving three terms of parliament. During her parliamentary career, Melissa was appointed parliamentary secretary for Mental Health, Homelessness and Social Housing and minister for International Development. Before this, Melissa worked as a senior lawyer in the United Nations for eight years, serving in Kosovo, Gaza, New York and Lebanon. Prior to joining the UN, she was a lecturer in law at Murdoch University and, before that, solicitor-in-charge at the Bunbury Community Legal Centre. She grew up in the South-West of WA on her parents' apple farm in Donnybrook.

Parsi grew up not far from Bassendean Oval, which made life very interesting with his being a dyed-in-the-wool East Perth supporter. He became a sannyasin in 1984 and an Eagles fan from day one of the club's foundation. He loves the local derbies and finds it remarkable how many of the Freo mob have a sudden urge to get in touch whenever they have a win – by phone, fax, text, email or carrier pigeon.

Janet Peters was born in January 1949, in Subiaco. She met her husband Allan in Alice Springs and they have two daughters. Peters lives in Northam and has worked at the Northam Regional Hospital for over thirty years. She loves travelling and has been to Europe, UK, NZ and Singapore and has seen quite a bit of Australia, with Tasmania being her favourite. She loves spending time with her family and going to see her beloved Eagles play, a team she has been a member of for twenty-five years.

John Prior is a barrister practising from Francis Burt Chambers Perth and has been a Commissioner of the Legal Aid Commission of WA since 2012. John has been a member of the Investigation Tribunal for Western Australian Amateur Football League since 1998. He has been legal counsel for the Fremantle Football Club since 1995 and provided legal advice to a number of WAFL clubs. He has also been a member and passionate supporter of Fremantle Football Club since the club started in 1995. John played 150 amateur league football games at a very low grade. He has coached both junior and amateur football teams. He has coached two premiership teams. He now plays Veterans hockey at a low standard.

Matt Quinn (aka Mr Q) is Perth born and bred, and has followed the Eagles since their inception in 1987. He has now been a member for twenty-five years, attending most games except for a few years when he lived in London and Sydney. An IT professional by trade, Matt set up the EaglesFlyingHigh.com website in 2004 to provide an internet presence for Eagles fans, and he has been running it ever since.

Kim Scott is a multi-award-winning novelist. Proud to be one among those who call themselves Noongar, he is founder and chair of the Wirlomin Noongar Language and Story Project (www.wirlomin.com.au). Kim is currently Professor of Writing at Curtin University.

Dr Glen Stasiuk is a lecturer and senior Indigenous researcher at Murdoch University and award-winning film director. Glen is a maternal descendent (Keen/Farmer/Hayward) of the Minang-Wadjari Noongars of the South-West of WA, while his paternal family immigrated from post-war Russia. These rich and varied cultural backgrounds have allowed him, through his filmmaking, research and writing, to explore culture, knowledge and diverse narratives.

Bill Sutherland has made a rich contribution to WA football over more than forty-five years. He was head trainer of the Central Wheatbelt Football Association (1964–75), also nine years as club president, and was made a life member in 1975. He was head trainer and president of the Dowerin Football Club, head trainer of the Mortlock Football Association (1976–77), before serving at Claremont Football Club (1978–86) as assistant head trainer. Bill became the head trainer at the West Coast Eagles Football Club from their inception in 1987 until 2007. He was an inaugural Hall of Fame inductee and was made a life member of the club in 1996. Sutherland received the national Jack Titus Award in 2006 for his services to football, the AFL Coaches Association Support Staff Leadership Award (2004) and the AFL Trainers Association Outstanding Service Award (2000). He received the Australian Sports Medal in 2000.

Bevan Taylor was born in the summer of '69 and raised on the family farm just west of Lake Grace. In year nine he was shipped off to boarding school where he quickly adjusted and thrived on the sporting culture of Aquinas College. Windsurfing and football consumed him as a young man until he met the love of his life, Maria, whom he married in 1990 and has four children whom he loves dearly. Despite years of toil he is still battling away on the farm trying to make things work. In his spare time Taylor likes to go hang-gliding and watching the greatest team in the world, the Eagles.

David Wirrpanda is a premiership player with the West Coast Eagles. Born in Melbourne, he was raised in Shepparton, Victoria, and later attended Worawa Aboriginal College in Healesville, which was established by his mother's family. Wirrpanda made his debut for West Coast in 1996. He played his first game for West Coast at the age of sixteen years and 268 days, the youngest player to have ever played a senior game for the club. An outstanding back man, he made the All-Australian team in 2005, and retired at the end of the 2009 season. He is married to Shannon McGuire and has three boys. Since the conclusion of his playing career he has been active in establishing the David Wirrpanda Foundation, an organisation supporting Indigenous Australians.

ACKNOWLEDGEMENTS

We would like to thank in the first instance our fathers. Tony Whish-Wilson, who played in the WAFL and other leagues, and who never showed his disappointment when his eldest son betrayed him by choosing to follow the Richmond Tiges over his beloved Bombers in the VFL, and later the Dockers, and who instilled the values of the game in the usual way – kick-to-kick down at the park (which mother Rosemary was also very good at). Thanks are due to Peter Gorman for turning Sean into a Claremont supporter. Without his abiding love for the Monts, Sean would never have followed Freo (it's a Neesham thing). To Sean's mum Annette for typing up all the interviews and making our job easier, many thanks. To Curtin University for making the transcriptions possible through the small grants scheme, thank you also. To the media men at the two Perth clubs – Gary Stocks and Luke Morfesse – thanks for all the contacts and for use of the clubrooms when requested. To all those friends who passed on the names and numbers of people with great stories or helped tee up interviews much thanks – especially to Janet and Don Pyke, Mark Constable, Aidan Kelly, Bevan Honey and Susannah Castleden. To all the great people we interviewed and spoke to about their love of the Eagles and the Dockers – a massive thanks. And last but by no means least to the many remarkable players who have graced that unremarkable oval called Subiaco and our television screens during those epic and sometimes not so epic games, thanks!

First published 2017 by
FREMANTLE PRESS
25 Quarry Street, Fremantle WA 6160
(PO Box 158, North Fremantle WA 6159)
www.fremantlepress.com.au

Statistics, pp. 220–22: <wikipedia.org/wiki/Western_Derby>

Editors David Whish-Wilson and Sean Gorman
Cover design Tracey Gibbs
Cover photograph © Printed by Everbest Printing Company, China

National Library of Australia
Cataloguing-in-Publication entry

Derby: WA footy fans on the game's greatest rivalry
Edited by Sean Gorman, David Whish-Wilson.

ISBN: 9781925164497 (paperback)

Subjects: Australian football—Western Australia.
Football fans—Western Australia—Interviews.
Sports rivalries—Western Australia.

Other Creators/Contributors:
Gorman, Sean, 1969– editor.
Whish-Wilson, David, editor.

Fremantle Press is supported by the State Government through the Department of Culture and the Arts